The *Moxie Mystique* tells how a patented nerve food—allegedly a cure for locomotor ataxia, inbecility, loss of manhood and much much more—spawned a name for the Spirit of America, a word for the audacity of the movers and shakers who continue to change the world. This book will delight readers with its heart-tugging backward glances toward a glittering bygone time when America was younger and wilder and when fewer holds were barred.

A mountain of memorabilia surrounds the storied Moxie Legend, here presented for the first time between covers: the bottle wagons, the bottle house, the Moxie songs, the weird and wonderful horsemobiles, the way The Moxie Company latched onto whatever was happening—including two world wars—to promote its product, which eventually became a very popular carbonated drink outselling Coca Cola.

Moxie left in its wake a treasure trove of collectibles which many soda-pop-art aficionados claim are superior to Coke's in quality and as investments—many of which are covered in detail in this fascinating and colorful book.

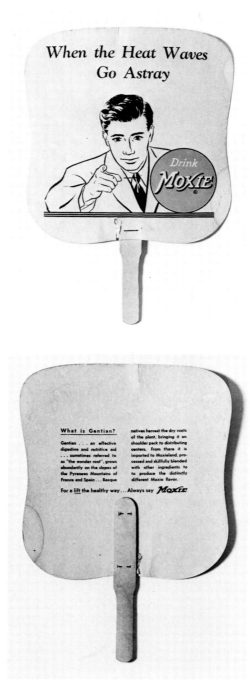

THE MOXIE MYSTIQUE

FRANK N. POTTER

Hank Stine, Editor

Copyright © 1981 by Frank N. Potter

Moxibooks
300 Clements Street
Paducah, Kentucky
42003-1437

**Library of Congress Cataloging in Publica-
tion Data**

Potter, Frank N., 1911-
    The Moxie Mystique.

    1. New England Moxie Company—
History.   I. Title.
HD9394.S63N486   338.7'66362'0974
    81-5499
ISBN 0-89865-145-X   AACR2

Printed in the United States of America

For my good friend
John N. Garrison III

Contents

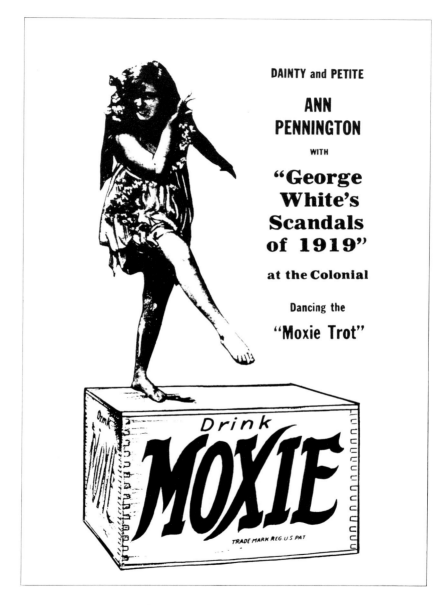

Preface

"To a Californian over 40," says Bill Gaylord, "the name Moxie sounds like the female character in a 1920's novel about New York. It conjures images of big, powerful cars driven by dashing, dark-eyed guys whose dolls knew all the right answers. Moxie was know-how. Moxie was courage. Moxie was daring."* The mystique of Moxie could hardly be better expressed.

Moxie is also a soft drink. It got its start over a hundred years ago as a bottled nerve food that uncorked an advertising phenomenon unmatched in this or any other country. Dr. Augustin Thompson couldn't have concocted his nostrum at a more promising time. The era was ripe for reaping. Laws were lax. People believed in what was happening. Moxie happened! And a man for that moment arrived in the person of Frank Morton Archer, an intrepid entrepreneur armed with hair-trigger charisma, wizardry and unbridled imagination. With a flair for showmanship—and prophesying profits galore—he gave magic to Moxie; put Moxie on the tongues of millions of his believers; produced showers of lapel buttons depicting Uncle Sam's hat, and the inscription: "What This Country Needs Is Plenty Of Moxie."

Hardly an event occurred that Moxie didn't latch on to. When America became involved in World War I, Moxie produced patriotic phonograph records. An officer of the United States Army Recruiting Service hit the streets astride a Moxie horsemobile. When the *Boston Post* newspaper had a banner headline announcing an eclipse of the sun in 1931, it also ran a three-column, front-page ad showing an immense bottle of Moxie under a Hall of Fame arch with a sign proclaiming "Moxie Eclipses Everything!"

*Reprinted with permission of *The Antiques Journal*, Dubuque Iowa.

This was the milieu in which Moxie made its bid for immortality and spawned a name for the spirit of America, a word for the audacity of the movers and shakers who continue to change the world—and for whom even the distant skies hold no limit. It is not enough for them to have faith in what they attempt; they need the moxie to do it.

This book tells how all this happened, how "moxie" came to mean what it does throughout our nation and, now, even on the moon. Hot dogs, baseball, apple pie and Chevrolet are fine as far as they go; but moxie goes deeper, wider, higher. Lets hope its mystique will never die.

Frank N. Potter
Newport News, VA

For
Syd Leach
Cordially

Frank N. Potter

CHAPTER 1

The Genie In the Bottle

Contains not a drop of Medicine, Poison, Stimulant or Alcohol. But is a simple sugarcane-like plant grown near the Equator and farther south, was lately accidentally discovered by Lieut. Moxie and has proved itself to be the only harmless nerve food known that can recover brain and nervous exhaustion; loss of manhood, imbecility and helplessness. It has recovered paralysis, softening of the brain, locomotor ataxia, and insanity when caused by nervous exhaustion. It gives a durable solid strength, makes you eat voraciously; takes away the tired, sleepy, listless feeling like magic, removes fatigue from mental and physical overwork at once, will not interfere with action of vegetable medicines.

. . .so claimed the label on a bottle of BEVERAGE MOXIE NERVE FOOD.

In 1555, when wicked Catherine de Medici's court physician, Nostradamus, was concocting nostrums and potions for his patroness, he predicted exciting possibilities in rhymed quatrains. Little did he dream that similar ditties would someday work wonders for the sale of a curious carbonated tonic derived from a Down East cure-all.

Long before folks became attuned to "Pepsi Cola hits the spot. . .," imbibers were singing the promotional praises of Moxie which, in its heyday, outsold even Coca Cola. When pretty young things carrying parasols, and dandies in celluloid collars, were swinging arm in arm to "Meet me in St. Louis, Louis," others were singing "Just Make It Moxie For Mine"—the first verse of which reminded them that, among "The sights you see there at the St. Louis fair," was a man in an apron selling Moxie.

But Moxie didn't hit the World's Fair of 1904 as something

1

new. It originated as a nostrum around 1876. By the turn of the century, it had become a soda pop with a strong medicinal taste and, somewhat bitter though it may have been, it went into strong competition with other thirst quenchers. The chorus of the Moxie "commercial" kept repeating: "Some take sarsparilla *(sic)* or beer that is pale, a glass of plain soda or else ginger ale, but just make it Moxie for mine." To reassure folks that Moxie was truly beneficial, the chorus went on to say that Moxie was "a drink they serve which will build up your nerve." The suggestion that soda pop can somehow be "good for you" still remains. As if its name were not enough, Dr. Pepper, that southern favorite, not long ago was "prescribing"—by the use of a clock face in its ads and embossed on its bottles—that you should drink it at certain hours during the day.

The main difference between a nostrum and a tonic is that some tonics may be quaffed as beverages (in a pinch, during Prohibition, even hair tonic was taken internally) whereas a nostrum is generally considered to be stronger and is usually spoon-fed. An overlap of these concepts often existed—as was reflected in the name Beverage Moxie Nerve Food.

How "nostrum," the Latin word for "ours," came to mean what it does in English is somewhat of a mystery. Perhaps it's because so many of these panaceas were eagerly accepted by the public. Moxie, in particular, became "ours" to a continuously loyal coterie of customers who, even today, take pride in calling themselves "Moxie Drinkers."

Webster's definition of "nostrum" as "a medicine of secret composition recommended by its preparer but usually lacking in general repute" leaves one wondering just how much the word "medicine" should honor. However, inasmuch as medicine can be construed to include magic potions produced by American Indians, a great many early cure-alls certainly qualify. As for how highly nostrums are regarded, we can but reflect upon the customer faith that still enables scores of concocters to become very rich indeed. One great binge that lasted almost twenty years began in 1947 when Louisiana Senator, The Honorable Dudley J. LeBlanc, dipped his Golden Oar into a barrel and stirred up a mixture containing twelve percent ethyl alcohol which he called Hadacol. Before Hadacol finally hit the skids, the redoubtable "Cousin Dud" had sold, in 1950 alone, some $24 million worth of his "dietary supplement."

Just make it MOXIE for mine

There are stories all over the country
Of women of song and of wine
The sights you see there at the St. Louis fair
Of the beach in the bright summer time.
But they're not in your thoughts for a minute
When your thirst makes you stand right in line
And the man in the apron says "What will
    you have?"
You say, "Just make it MOXIE for mine."

When the summer time comes and vacation
Which with your best girl you will share
A trip you will take to the beach or the lake,
And make both hearts feel happy while there.
Then you take in the dance hall and
    pleasures
And her eyes with a sparkle do shine
When you say with a wink, "Come girl let's
    have a drink"
She says "Just make it MOXIE for mine."

Copyrighted in 1904 by the Moxie Nerve Food Company of New England. Lyrics by W. P. Mitchell; music by Bert Potter. When this sheet music was issued, the Moxie Company had not yet decided on a standard logotype. The "X" in the song's title has its crossbar looped differently than it did later on.

LeBlanc's original method of mixing his Hadacol is strikingly similar to the way Lonesome Polecat used to stir up his potent tubful of Kickapoo Joy Juice in Al Capp's "Lil Abner" comic strip. Kickapoo Joy Juice (as late as 1977) was the name of a soft drink produced by The Monarch Company, a subsidiary of Moxie Industries of Atlanta, Georgia, which also markets the new Moxie. At one time, Kickapoo was an Indian Salve made from healing herbs and bark, "a perfect cure-all in Skin Diseases—for various forms of Tetter, Erisipelas, Scald Head, Barber's Itch, Corns and Burns and Itching Piles."

It wasn't obligatory, of course, for a patent palliative to be developed from a secret Indian recipe; still, there's no doubt that such a claim could help sell all sorts of snake oil. Although most nostrums were sold through stores and mail order houses, many were hawked in the boondocks from the backs of the vehicles in which they were bottled—some still are.

The woods may no longer be full of Indians, but more than a few of these native Americans were once highly visible as stock-in-trade standbys of medicine shows. No peddler of panaceas with wampum on his mind was likely to sally forth in his caravan without at least one Redskin in eagle feathers and beads to bestow blessings on the believers who bought the magic waters —or put the Injun Sign on the doubters who held onto their dollars.

No record has come to light indicating that the New England Moxie Company ever ran such a show, but the Indian inference was, willy-nilly, in its name. Many Massachusetts folk, whose forebears had taken an Indian name (meaning People of the Great Hill Country) for their Commonwealth, knew that down in Maine the mysterious Moxie Falls, steeped in Indian lore, tumbled its sparkling waters in a stream that emptied into the Kennebec (Long Water Land) River; that there was a Moxie Cove in Round Pond, Maine, near Damariscotta (River of Little Fishes); and that somewhere else in Maine deer came to drink from Moxie Pond hidden among the hills where moxie berry and moxie plum grow.

Although Moxie appears to be of Indian origin, the product may very well have derived its name from another source. When Mrs. Virginia McElwee, granddaughter of Dr. Augustin Thompson, the inventor of Moxie, was asked where Moxie got its name, she replied: "As far as I know, for a friend of grandfather's. I never heard it told many times." To which Ivy Dodd, a writer for the Rockland, Maine, *Courier-Gazette,* added: "Perhaps, who knows,

attention

MOXIE ®

drinkers

AS DRINKERS OF _MOXIE_ YOU KNOW THAT:
- *Moxie* is the trademark of one of the oldest soft drinks ... first bottled in 1884.
- *Moxie* is a tradition in New England.
- *Moxie* has always been different and distinctive in taste.

A GREAT NEW _MOXIE_ TASTE IS COMING SOON
- It is coming to stores in your area.
- You'll see *Moxie* in bright new red and yellow packages.

TRY THIS REFRESHING NEW TASTE OF _MOXIE_
- You'll find the new taste of *Moxie* different and distinctive ... as *Moxie* has always been.

MOXIE HAS A TASTE ALL ITS OWN!
- We thank you for being a drinker of *Moxie* . We hope you'll continue to be a *Moxie* drinker for many years to come.

THE _MOXIE_ COMPANY
— and —
YOUR LOCAL _MOXIE_ BOTTLER

7-UP BOTTLING CO. OF NEW BEDFORD
INDUSTRIAL PARK, NEW BEDFORD, MASS.
MOXIE IS THE REGISTERED TRADEMARK OF THE _MOXIE_ COMPANY

The logotype trade mark used in this mid-1960s ad was first registered in 1907; it is the one used today.

it was someone Dr. Thompson had known in his Army days." And Mrs. Dodd hadn't seen that old Moxie bottle label with the name of "Lieutenant Moxie" on it. And again, who knows, could "Lieutenant Moxie" perhaps have been an Indian?

Patented nostrums were sold during the lifetimes of folks who could recall the American Revolution. As early as 1840, cure-all promoters were providing free advertising almanacs. It was after the Civil War, however, that the great bamboozle blossomed into full flower. From 1870 until after the Pure Food and Drug Act of 1906 was passed forbidding unsubstantiated claims for products marketed across state lines, a plethora of proprietary pap was guzzled by the gullible in vast quantities.

The 1902 Sears Roebuck catalog—together with advertisements for Heidelberg Electric Belts which allegedly cured all female weaknesses, impotency in men, and other ailments in men caused by "excesses, indiscretions, etc."—contained six pages listing more than a score of "cures" in various forms. An entire page—with a picture of a naked Sampson pulling apart the jaws of a struggling lion—was devoted to Vin Vitae, the Wine of Life, retailing at $1.25 a pint, but sold by Sears for only sixty-nine cents.

Although its claims were not quite as preposterous as Moxie's, Vin Vitae was also strongly recommended as a pepper-upper and nerve tonic. As a competitor, if not downright imitator of Moxie, Vin Vitae was promoted as containing "all the good properties of all well known sarsaparillas, blood purifiers, regulators for men and women, nerve tonics, etc. without their disagreeable and distasteful ingredients."

Whether or not making a medicine taste good may have been of some advantage, many folks felt that medicine should taste like medicine to be effective; and Moxie had a bitter enough flavor to satisfy these customers. Furthermore, Moxie cost only twenty-five cents for almost a quart. Vin Vitae, however, was well laced with the "finest wines of sunny California."

What the original Moxie Nerve Food tasted like is a matter of some conjecture. Projected on a backward curve based on what reports say the various later Moxie tonic flavors were like, we can assume that the nerve food must have tasted very medicinal indeed. In their Morris Dictionary of Word and Phrase Origins, William and Mary Morris mistakenly hazarded a guess that the present meaning of the word "moxie" probably came about because "the original *Moxie* was so bitter that you had to have plenty of courage to drink the stuff.''

But bitter isn't necessarily all that unappetizing. Many drinkers relish a dash or two of Angustora Bitters in their cocktails; others ask for Schweppes or Canada Dry Bitter Lemon or quinine Tonic Water in their highballs; and, in England, beer drinkers often prefer bitters to mild.

Not every proprietary medicine was promoted as a cure-all. Many were sold for special purposes. Hostetter's Celebrated Stomach Bitters was for indigestion; Cures Celery, for constipation; Imperial Granum, for diseases of the stomach and intestines; Phenix, for your nerves; Ayer's Sarsaparilla claimed to cure chronic fatigue; Egyptian Regulator Tea was supposed to give ''graceful plumpness'' to girls' bosoms; and Rengo, for men, was just the thing to ''turn fat into muscle.'' Hundreds more cured everything from warts to worms.

Whatever the alleged functions of the various nostrums that appeared on the market from the Civil War until after World War I, most of the more successful cure-alls—like the later Hadacol—had one common operative ingredient, operative in the sense that it was responsible for sales on its own account. It must be remembered that the Prohibition movement was well under way during this period; and many a self-respecting citizen who wouldn't dream of buying booze per se had no compunctions about visiting the local apothecary and carting home several bottles of The Original Syrup of Black Draught, alcohol 5%; Swamp Root (courtesy of S. Andral Kilmer, M.D.), alcohol 10½; Cardui (with an Indian on the label), alcohol 19%; or Paine's Celery Compound, alcohol 21%! A sweetened cure-all containing alcohol is classified as an elixir.

Peruna, containing 15% alcohol, was an exceedingly popular favorite during Prohibition. The cognoscenti—perhaps because the stuff could weave a web of dreams—nicknamed it ''Spider.'' The early Peruna was promoted as having great medicinal value. According to interested authorities, so the legend goes, indeed it had not any! The Peruna people then conscientiously, but without announcing it on their label, invested their tonic with a scruple of laxative. There followed an epidemic of ''the mulligrubs,''—what has been jocularly referred to by puzzled physicians as The Year of the Great Borborygmous (borborygmous: a medical term meaning a rumbling sound made by the movement of gas in the intestine).

Why so many tonics were permitted to stay on the market

when they were obviously consumed solely for their alcoholic content is a moot question perhaps best answered by the Commissioner of Internal Revue in 1883 when he said: "To draw the line nicely, and fix definitely where the medicine may end and the alcoholic beverage begin, is a task which has often perplexed and still perplexes revenue officers."

Vanilla extract was often sold for other than flavoring during this period. A woman who bought a small grocery store in New Hampshire, and found that the inventory included several shelves full of Jamaica ginger and cases of the stuff in the storeroom, thought that the previous owner had been sold a bill of goods. Her first day behind the counter, however, convinced her otherwise. She soon learned what was wanted when customer after customer came in asking for a bottle of "jake." Unfortunately, Jamaica ginger drinking produced a type of paralysis commonly known as "jake leg."

Many of the curative products mentioned so far, as well as several other standbys such as non-alcoholic Lydia Pinkham's Vegetable Compound, may still be found on drug store shelves. Around 1970, an inspection of the labels on these concoctions revealed that they contained one or more of the following: *Roots*— gentian, oregon grape, blood, queen's, pleurisy, life, blue cohosh, black cohosh, rhubarb, mandrake, valerian and columbo; *bark*— wild cherry and cascara; *oils*—juniper and birch; *balsams*—copaiba and tolu; *other* (unidentified as to plant part)—Jamaica dogwood, black haw, licorice, cinnamon, dandelion, cape aloes, golden seal and blessed thistle.

The Moxie formula, allegedly a well-kept secret, underwent several changes over the years. It was generally reported as simply "a bitterish concoction of gentian-root extract and about twenty other flavors." A fountain syrup label, however, listed the contents as containing water, sugar, cinchona alkaloids, caramel and flavoring. Cinchona is a bitter bark from South America and contains quinine, which is used to reduce fever. On the other hand, sassafras (formerly Moxie's chief flavoring agent) is used to induce perspiration. One of the main objectives of the Lost Colonists— who sailed from England to Roanoke Island in the summer of 1587—was to collect sassafras, which was being promoted as a great new remedy for all ills. Sassafras, it seems, may have other effects. In 1960, the Pure Food and Drug Administration outlawed the use of sassafras in food and drinks for health reasons. On April

27, 1978, Ruth Beeler White, Ph.D., director of consumer inquiries, Department of Health, Education and Welfare, wrote: "Because safrole and oil of sassafras are carcinogens, sassafras tea can no longer be transported in interstate commerce."

Sassafras Tea

From root, through wood, to bloom, the sassafras
Keeps its consistence of fragrance still,
Though few may recognize it as they pass
Its valiant growth from ledges on the hill.
But it had steamed from many cups before
These days, an aromatic breath to tweak
The doubter's nose—till he demanded more
With tongue beguiled and tingles in the cheek.
Old flavors lost we must now find again,
Renewing hardy guests of earlier years
That toughened fibers, gave to women and men
The gamey tastes that nourished pioneers.
Soon many more may cherish, with the few,
Earth-flavors richer in this native brew.

—Glen Ward Dresbach

Moxie was "exposed" in a 1903 book, *The Secrets of the Specialists*, in which a Dr. Dale Covey claimed that "despite the wonderful tale of its discovery, and although so 'wholly unknown to botonists,' Moxie is, we presume to say, a plant known as avena sativa. The great 'Nerve Food' is a decoction of oats made into a syrup and flavored with sassafras and wintergreen." The fountain syrup label, incidentally, depicts a skirt-clad reaper carrying a sickle and shouldering a sheaf of what could be oats. Is she merely Mother Ceres, the Roman deity of agriculture, or is she the Moxie Goddess about to surprise the footloose Lieutenant with a sample of that "simple sugarcane-like plant grown near the Equator?"

What, then, made non-alcoholic Moxie so popular? For the most part, Moxie's success was due to the advertising genius of a certain Frank Archer—one trick of whose was to hail Moxie as a substitute for whiskey. Because drivers who were fast switching to a fascinating new invention called the horseless carriage were finding that they could no longer have one too many and trust to the horse to get them safely home, Archer began to plug Moxie

The Moxie Goddess appearing on this label was also used on the early, paper, bottle labels.

"For Safe Driving" as the perfect "one for the road," pick-me-up with a punch that wouldn't knock you out. Beyond their alcohol-and-gasoline-don't-mix theme, the Moxie Company also reminded folks of the evils of liquor under any circumstances, and much to the delight of the Women's Christian Temperance Union, produced the New England Cure for Alcoholism. It must have pleased the Prohibitionists plenty to know that what had once been an immense brewery was now Moxieland.

A teetotaler with a purpose was Miles Harold Carpenter of Buffalo, New York. When young "Hal" was hardly fourteen years old, he was hired by the George N. Pierce Company, which was later to produce the famous Pierce Arrow. In 1903, however, this company was building one-cylinder Pierce Motorettes and having some difficulty with them. Such was the nerve of this Carpenter kid that he let it be known that someday he'd make a really good machine—not just another cranky corn popper, but a fine motorcar.

"When I started work at Pierce," says Hal, "Charlie Sheppy (Pierce's Superintendent of Construction) gave me a word of advice about alcohol. He said that many big men in the automobile business were two-fisted drinkers, but drink had already knocked out more than one of them. He told me that if I stayed away from booze I could become a good automotive engineer and go places. But success in the automobile business took more than merely being a teetotaler and a good engineer; it took a lot of 'moxie.'"

An old-time institution—one that helped young Hal stretch his weekly pay of three silver dollars and a half-dollar piece—flourished along Lake Erie's industrial waterfront. As Hal describes it: "When the twelve-o'clock whistle blew, there was a mad rush to the nearest saloon. With a nickel drink, we were dished up a great plate of the best-cooked victuals. Each Monday we had roast beef; on Tuesday, beef hash. Friday was always fish day. On Saturday we got sauerkraut and weiners, all we could eat. Most of the men had big schooners of beer. A few took coffee. I drank Moxie. Some of the men ordered a second drink. That's where the house made its money.

"On the way home from work, I had to pass the intersection of Niagara and Main—just about the busiest spot in Buffalo. Thousands of people changed trolley cars there. What I recall most vividly about Niagara Square is the little Italian who used to hawk papers. He was a circus all by himself, making faces and clowning as he cried the news in an immense voice. His energy was fantastic. Folks nicknamed him 'Moxie.'"

Interestingly, just before twenty-nine-year-old Hal Carpenter bought the prestigious Phianna Motor Car Company—and proceeded to redesign it and make it "America's Representative Among the World's Finest Cars"—he mounted a harness maker's dummy horse on a Dort automobile chassis for the Moxie Company of Boston. This contraption was driven from the horse's saddle and created quite a stir wherever it appeared. It was one of the various eye-catching Moxie advertising vehicles which did so much to promote Moxie's success.

But it took more than advertising to make Moxie tonic popular. It had to taste good if you were to drink it like ginger ale, and somehow it did—after you got used to it. Some folks could never learn to drink the stuff; said it tasted like Lavoris with a dash of onion; but they were a minority. Actually, you might be inclined to spit out your first mouthful of that old Moxie. A moment later, though, you'd probably try another sip.

A three-foot-high placard recently found in the attic of Albert Harjula's house in Thomaston, Maine, first appeared around 1908 or earlier. Lettering on wooden Moxie cases depicted on this placard, "Learn to Drink Moxie, Very Healthful," reflects that Moxie was an acquired taste, but that it was good for you. Lettering on some wooden Moxie cases contained innocuous messages like, "Drink Moxie, It's Always a Pleasure to Serve You." This phrase seems to have been a favorite of The Moxie Company, for it was still being used even in the late 1960s on small Dixie cups supplied for sampling Moxie at sales promotion exhibits. Moxie's wooden cases were eventually imprinted simply, "Drink Moxie."

The label on a bottle of Moxie also shown on this placard says that it is the product of The Moxie Nerve Food Company of New England, Boston and New York; guaranteed under the Food and Drug Act of June 30, 1906. Although Moxie bottle labels were, by then, omitting some of their earlier, more preposterous claims, this label does contain passages such as: "As a household beverage to counteract the exhausting effects of life and as an aid in preventing the weakening effects of weather upon the system, it is very beneficial."

There was something about the old Moxie that certainly was "Distinctly Different!" There's never been another drink anything like it. This early Moxie tonic got up into your nose like horse radish and made you snort. It was a wall-banger long before Harvey arrived. Today, the flavor is less startling but, alas, Moxie no longer outsells Coca Cola. As Bob Considine, the popular

Large cutouts, such as this "feather tickle" poster, were widely displayed and often appeared on the running boards of the early Moxie autos.

columnist, asked a few years ago: "Whatever happened to that great thirst quencher of my youth, Moxie?"

The camaraderie that developed among Moxie drinkers was a

The machine-turned finish used on the hood, fenders, etc. of this 1917 Dort Moxiemobile reflects the craftsmanship employed in its construction. This is the only known photograph showing a Moxiemobile used, even temporarily, to advertise any product other than Moxie.

tonic-maker's dream. The owner of an ancient bottling plant in Massachusetts claims that there's an informal Moxie Drinkers Club in town that still depends on him for its supply. He furnishes "old-fashioned" Moxie to them free. Some of them drink Moxie

The Moxie Company's first horsemobile—obviously not driven from the saddle, although a passenger could ride on it. Western as well as English saddles were used on various Moxiemobiles.

Mroczka, a mixture of Moxie and milk. Frank Anicetti, Jr., a fruit dealer in Lisbon Falls, Maine, signs his letters "A Moxie Drinker." When word arrived that Moxie might be distributed nation-wide once more, one senior citizen in California exclaimed: "If I wasn't too old, I'd jump for joy that Moxie will be with us again."

Loyalty to Moxie—even to the legend of Moxie—knows no bounds. An English lady now making her home in New England and fascinated by its traditions recently said: "I just wish I could learn to like the taste of Moxie!" Why? Maybe because Moxie is really more American than apple pie.

> Oh, give me the sassafras, nurse,
> and the juniper juice,
> and then turn me loose;
> let me see if I'm still any use!
> Anon.

CHAPTER 2

A Soldier of Fortune

On November 25, 1835—the year bearbaiting was banned in England—Augustin Thompson made his appearance on this planet. He might have pursued any of a number of careers. Circumstances certainly provided him with many avenues for his burgeoning proclivities. The Fates, however, conspired to make him a man of medicine. His granddaughter, Mrs. Virginia McElwee—who still lives on the family homestead in Union, Maine—remembers him well.

"Grandfather was a dynamic man," says Virginia. "He was always full of new ideas, always trying something. Many years later, when the 'plenty of moxie' phrase was used in a play I saw in New York, I thought how pleased he would have been; for he was always interested in the theater himself. In fact, one of the plays Grandfather wrote was the first one that Maurice Barrymore, father of John, Lionel and Ethel, appeared in in this country."

According to *Union (Maine) Past and Present,* published in 1895, "He (Augustin Thompson) is well informed, has travelled extensively and always with his eyes open, a man of ideas with the courage to put them in practice, a miniature steam engine in energy and vital force, and who would succeed in making himself felt in any enterprise in which he might embark."

As a young man Mr. Thompson farmed in Union with his family, then moved to Rockland where he made barrels for the lime plants in Thomaston, doing some blacksmithing on the side. When the Civil War came, young Augustin rallied a group of volunteers and enlisted with them as a private. He was promoted rapidly and was twice recommended in the field. During the war, no doubt as a result of the wounds he and his comrades suffered, he decided to become a doctor. After he was invalided out of the service, with the rank of Lieutenant Colonel, he waited just long enough for his bad lung to heal before enrolling in medical school, graduating from the Hahneman Hospital in Philadelphia.

At about this time, according to Mrs. McElwee, her grandfather was supervising the construction of Fort Popham at the mouth of the Kennebec River. It is still there. "Mother told me that Grandmother went by stage to Bath, after which soldiers rowed her in an open boat with her baby in her arms to spend Christmas there with her husband."

The new doctor Thompson and a fellow graduate decided that Lowell, Massachusetts would be a likely place to set up practice. The mills were booming then. Over the next twenty years Dr. Thompson built up a fine practice there. Incidentally, Lowell happened to be the home of three famous patent medicines (Lydia Pinkham lived in nearby Lynn) which were selling widely, especially in South America where doctors were scarce. The success of these patented potions was certainly something the enterprising Dr. Thompson could not ignore.

In 1876, he mixed up a concoction of gentian-root extract and some other ingredients and called it Moxie Nerve Food. This was a concentrated liquid to be taken by the spoonful immediately before meals as an aid to digestion. It was guaranteed to make you eat better, sleep better, feel better. Gentian was well known before Moxie came along. Indeed, it was legendary.

Gentius, an Illyrian king, was defeated by the Romans in 161 B.C. Wounded, he took refuge in the Roman (Italian) Alps. Surrounding the cave in which he hid from the Romans were plants that produced beautiful flowers, both blue and yellow in hue. Gentius, besides admiring the beauty of these plants, ate the roots and was returned to health. Upon his eventual arrival in his homeland, Gentius had with him specimens of this extraordinary plant, which botonists then named in his honor.

As with all legends, there is usually some dispute. The gentian whose roots are used for medicinal purposes do not have blue flowers, only yellow. However, there grows, in New England, a bottle gentian whose flowers are blue. But this gentian got its name from the fact that the blossoms do not open fully and resemble bottles; it was not named after bottled Moxie. Incidentally, Good King Gentius lived to the ripe old age of eighty-seven—which may, perhaps, speak well for his peculiar herbal diet, bitter though it may have been.

For several years Doctor Thompson proceeded to produce his Moxie Nerve Food, together with Moxie Catarrh Cure—in a little clear glass flask only an inch and a half in diameter—and The New England Cure for Alcoholism—all of which gained considerable credence with customers and became household names.

By 1884, Dr. Thompson became impressed by the progress and evident financial success of the carbonated beverages then making their appearance; so he began to produce what he called Beverage Moxie Nerve Food, "a delicious blend of the bitter and the sweet, a drink to satisfy everyone's tastes." "I never knew exactly what Grandfather put in his Nerve Food," Mrs. McElwee admits. "I was only four when he died—but I do know that gentian roots and sassafras went into it, with soda water and certain herbs, the kind that people used for herb teas in those days."

But Dr. Thompson didn't want folks to think that he was simply turning out a soda pop flavored to taste somewhat like his original medicine. He stressed the care and patience required to produce his "improved" product, and the fact that one had to get used to drinking it by the glassful. The making of Moxie "can not be hurried," he insisted. "It takes exactly ten days to extract the flavor from the gentian root. Many have said: 'When I first tasted Moxie, I didn't like it. When I had taken one or two glasses, served ice cold, I found it to be delicious and satisfying.'"

Frank M. Archer, who had joined Dr. Thompson and was instrumental in the very successful advertising of Moxie, explained why the product was changed from a by-the-spoonful medicine to a tonic for by-the-glassful consumption. In the early 1900s, Frank Archer stated: "The late Dr. Augustin Thompson, the originator of Moxie, discovered through his enormous practice, the necessity of a beverage which could be used freely, one with true tonic qualities, a pure food and supreme thirst quencher and appetizer, healthful and refreshing, pure, harmless, and absolutely free from any deleterious ingredients, to meet the wants of both young and old."

The "true tonic qualities" of Beverage Moxie Nerve food, however, did supposedly accomplish great things for those who drank it—as we have already seen from claims on one of the labels. Be that as it may, when push came to shove with the passage of the Pure Food and Drug Act of 1906, Moxie was found to be quite innocent, in content, at least.

This rare old photograph was taken in Lowell, Mass., back when each bottle of Moxie came neatly wrapped in paper. The strange vehicle behind the wagon is perhaps the very first of the Moxie Bottle Wagons. Note the Moxie Goddess depicted on the bottle. To her left is an American flag, symbolic of Moxie's continuing patriotic theme. In this photograph belonging to Mrs. Virginia McElwee, granddaughter of Dr. Augustin Thompson, two of his sons appear. Frank E. Thompson (later president of The Moxie Company) is seated to the right on the bottle wagon. Harry A. Thompson (later secretary-treasurer of The Moxie Company) is the short fellow standing in front of the wagon wheel; he was Mrs. McElwee's father.

But praise was never lacking in regard to Moxie's vaunted prowess. In 1895, *Union Past and Present* said this about Dr.

Thompson's product: "It is safe to say no article or compound, whether known as a medicine, food or by any other name, has made such gigantic strides into popularity and in such an incredibly short space of time. At this time even the doctor, sanguine in temperament though he is, scarce dreamed the phenomenal success soon to be achieved by it . . . Branch factories have been established in different parts of the country, until now there exists scarce a city from Halifax to San Francisco where 'Moxie' is unknown or has not been used. (It is) artificially digested and made ready for absorption before being taken into the system and to this is due Moxie's success where other nerve foods have failed—a secret known only to the doctor and one which skilled lawyers in court examinations have been unable to make him divulge.

"The success of this company has prompted spurious imitations and counterfeits of the genuine Nerve Food, but the doctor has pursued them with so much vigor that of late they have given him a wide berth. This Company is destined to be one of the massive corporations of the country. Moxie is already a household word in two hemispheres."

Moxie advertising was soon to become as well known as the product itself, not only in Maine but everywhere Moxie was sold. Of the many items used to promote Moxie, the most unusual were the Moxie vehicles—naturals for camera buffs. An 1886 shutterbug snapped a picture of what appears to be a Lowell, Massachusetts delivery of Moxie, each bottle neatly wrapped in a twist of paper. Behind the delivery cart is a rig carrying a gigantic replica of a Moxie bottle. This eye-catcher and later Moxie advertising vehicles always attracted crowds and business wherever they went.

On September 16, 1908, the Rockland (Maine) *Courier-Gazette* told its readers: "The covered automobile which appeared in town the latter part of the week is used to advertise the Moxie Company, and was under the charge of G. F. Ordway, who in the past nine months has toured the Atlantic coast from Norfolk, Va. to Rockland." No mean feat in those days, considering the condition of the roads.

The greatest attention-getter of all was the Moxie Horsemobile (later called simply the Moxiemobile), which consisted of a life-size, white, dummy horse mounted on an automobile chassis. Although this novel vehicle was patented in 1917, one had been constructed a year or so earlier and had soon become a well known moving landmark for Moxie. In its September 23, 1916, edition,

Although the sale of Moxie is now limited mostly to the New England area, it used to be distributed in thirty-seven states and, at one time, outsold Coca Cola.

The Cambridge Chronical had this to say: "The most unique thing of all the achievements in the advertising line undertaken by the Moxie Company was the creation of the now famous and wonderful Moxie Horsemobile, the joining of the horse and the automobile in a motor contraption that is ornamental, ingenious and wonderful. It certainly is a magnet that allures and people can hardly keep their eyes off from it."

The Rockland *Courier-Gazette* recorded a Moxiemobile visit in its edition of June 29, 1917: "The famous Moxie horse automobile visited Rockland Wednesday and attracted as much attention as a circus parade...Joseph E. King of Bangor is the jockey, and has been handling the Moxie horse for the past two years, during which he traveled over 10,000 miles. The horse has received more publicity than any advertising feature ever designed. On this trip through Maine, thousands of ornamented china ash trays, fans, and little balloons and lollipops for the children are being distributed."

In discussing the history of her grandfather's nerve food project, Mrs. McElwee was reminded that, when the Pure Food and Drug Act was passed in 1906, patent medicines, like everything else, came under considerable scrutiny and, since Moxie was classified as simply a soft drink and nothing more, the company eventually changed its name from The Moxie Nerve Company to The Moxie Company. The product, which had first been named Moxie Nerve Food, was called Beverage Moxie Nerve Food for a while, then simply Moxie.

Although the product may have been found to be nothing more than a soft drink, one ad for "The Famous MOXIE NERVE FOOD" had contained such passages as: "A Delicious and Healthful Beverage which is of greatest value to all persons suffering from Nervous Exhaustion and Incipient Paralysis. It has a very high reputation throughout the United States and is often prescribed by physicians of high standing. Avoid worthless imitations. Get the GENUINE ONLY. For sale by Druggists and Grocers." This ad also reminded folks that they could get "Beautiful souvenirs free at the Moxie Exhibition at the Pharmacy Fair."

"Some soft drinks using coca had to change their formulas," Mrs. McElwee continued. "Coca contains caffeine, of course, and those that contained a lot of it had to cut down on the quantity used." Moxie relied on its herbs for its tonic qualities, however, and contained no caffeine. Its color came from caramelized sugar and from the herbs.

"Just about the beginning of the Depression of the 1930s," Mrs. McElwee remembered, "we felt that the company should be expanded into a national one, but that was the wrong time, and we decided to sell the company altogether. Father and his brother, Frank, were getting along in years by then and they'd gotten all they wanted out of it. We had always bottled our goods ourselves and didn't sell the syrup to be put up by bottlers, but freight rates went up after World War I and it was hard to maintain Moxie as a five-cent drink. It was always sold for five cents a glass, so much the bottle and so much the case."

In 1952, Augustin's son Francis (Frank) had the Thompson Memorial Building erected in Union in memory of his father. It was to have been built earlier but the project had been delayed because of World War II. After the war, inasmuch as schools were urgently needed, the Thompson Memorial was designed as a combined school and town house. It contains a large gymnasium; and town meetings and town business are conducted there.

March 28, 1933

There is now a Moxie Deal on both Bottled Goods and Syrup.

See your Moxie Jobber or one of our salesmen at once.

THE MOXIE COMPANY

CHAPTER 3

Moxie
Makes Itself
Known

An old advertising cliche claims that "Nothing beats word of mouth." Some firms attempt to prime the pump by handing out stickers that read, "Tell a Friend About Bertha's Beautiful Beans" or whatever. This is usually a waste of good bumper space. Nobody is going to tell someone else about a product unless there's something good to say—or something bad, for that matter.

What it boils down to is that folks certainly do talk about anything that's different. Even if they bad-mouth a product, it's better than not having it talked about at all; and that's the way it worked for Moxie. Somebody might tell a friend that Moxie tastes terrible. Well, people may be highly influenced by someone else's preferences in clothes; but when it comes to tastes in food or drink, individuality is very much a matter of pride.

The next best thing to claiming that you're the only one on earth who likes a particular drink is to belong to a clique with a particular taste. Moxie never played down the fact that it had a bitter flavor. What Moxie did was to take a caviar-to-the-general approach, to turn its taste to an advantage. The pitch was that it took an enviable degree of sophistication to appreciate the taste of Moxie. Slogans such as, "It's the drink for those who are at all particular," began to appear. In a sort of reverse-word-of-mouth maneuver, Moxie had the very popular, successful and unquestionably individualistic Ed Wynn announce—from ads and posters showing him with a glass of Moxie in his hand—"I may be 'A Perfect Fool' but I'm *very particular.*"

Earlier, without actually getting a first-hand plug from a prominent personage, Moxie had taken a tack that backed its product into the limelight by reminding folks of a hero whose lifestyle reflected the zest that the word "moxie" was coming to mean. During the administration of that bully guy, Theodore

"I may be 'A Perfect Fool'" but I'm <u>very</u> particular"

Ed. Wynn

In The Grab Bag ~ appearing at the Tremont Theatre under the direction of A. L. Erlanger

Phone your dealer to deliver a case today

When Ed Wynn gave his long-time friend, Frank Archer, a promised fur coat, the presentation was made with much fanfare at Boston's Colonial Theater. The garment, enclosed in many wrappings within a large wooden packing case, turned out to be barely big enough to cover a bottle of Moxie.

Roosevelt, Moxie pointed to him as personifying the type that, today, is referred to as "macho." In an advertising broadside, Moxie told people who wanted to be like grinning Teddy that: "If you wish to live a strenuous life and be able to perform its duties cheerfully and vigorously, you will find Moxie Nerve Food a great help. Remember that alcohol, tobacco, coffee and other nerve stimulants tear down the nerve tissues, while Moxie builds up and supports the strenuous life."

Thus, Moxie put down a base of proud Moxie Drinkers who, with a little help from the folks in The Moxie Company, made Moxie drinking the "in thing." When Moxie eventually began to outsell Coca Cola, this didn't diminish the way Moxie drinkers felt about themselves. Their distinction shone even greater. They had become, in effect, charter members. They now sat back smiling with their thumbs in their vests. Hadn't they, after all, started the whole trend?

Praise from the business world and especially from the medical profession, then as now, was thought to have considerable clout. Moxie, it seemed, should no longer belong only in the home and at soda fountains and on picnics; it should be handy in offices and hospitals as well. An ad—complete with the Moxie Kid hefting a "Carrying Bag devised by F.M. Archer exclusively for Moxie, Reg. and Copyrighted;" and the Moxie Dog fetching a sign saying, "If at all particular;" and also bearing an announcement that Moxie was now available in three sizes of bottles—had this to say:

A well-known Boston business man at a recent conference told Frank Archer the following story:

> Last summer I was taken seriously ill and during the hot spell I was convalescing at the hospital. One day a famous surgeon arrived to perform an extremely difficult operation. After he had completed his trying task, I heard him enter the corridor, puffing and perspiring and calling for the nurse. When the nurse hastened to him, he said: "Phew, it's hot! I'm all fagged out. Do you happen to have any Moxie on hand?" Curious to see the noted specialist, I looked into the corridor just as the nurse returned with a glass and a bottle of Moxie. "That," he said, "is the most refreshing and invigorating beverage I can drink when I am tired and thirsty." I agreed with

him; for I have been a MOXIE enthusiast for years.
Order a case now, from your dealer, for your
office or home.

Another effective way to convince folks to buy a product is to scare them into becoming customers. Mature citizens, however, aren't easily frightened into changing their shopping habits; but they are inclined to try new products they have been convinced will help them with their real or imagined infirmities. Moxie's cure-all pitch had been highly successful with these people; they seemed to have gone quite willingly with Moxie from the spoon-fed nerve food to great draughts of the new tonic with the old familiar taste.

Kids were something else. Parents, even before the advent of today's so-called permissiveness, had often experienced a lamentable lack of persuasion when it came to the "drink this!" department. And parents couldn't be everywhere; but Moxie could be...well...almost everywhere. Moxie did it by dreaming up one of the most persuasive posters ever to meet the eye—and putting it just about any place the law allowed.

Meet the eye was exactly what this poster did. On it, was the picture of a handsome young man pointing. A bit of a smile was on his lips but those eyes were dead serious. He made girls blush and boys scuff and push their hands deeper into their pockets—where they just might find a nickel or two for some Moxie.

If you think this Moxie poster may have resembled that highly effective "Uncle Sam Needs You!" one which followed, Moxie graciously bows. Moxie was certainly American in spirit, and in action as well. Even its horse went to war. An officer in the U.S. Army Recruiting Service hit the streets astride a Moxie Horsemobile bearing signs that read "DO IT NOW!" Naturally, the Moxie signs on this vehicle were not covered up. But back to that Moxie Man poster. Let's hear from someone who recalls how it was. In an article published in 1970, Dallas Mundy had this to say:

"When I was too old for three-cornered pants but too young for grammar school (that's what they called elementary schools back when drug stores were known as apothecaries and a railway station was a depot), Perkin's window displayed a cardboard cutout picture of a wonderful-looking young man in an immaculate white jacket, and he pointed right at me. What made him even more awesome were high eyes. No matter where I stood, those true-blue eyes kept peering smack into mine. Man! I believed! When I got to grammar school and learned to read, I discovered that the words beside the conscience-stirring man's picture said 'Drink Moxie!' As far as I was concerned, he could just as well have been saying 'Thou Shalt' ahead of it."

THE MOXIE HORSEMOBILE
Shown in use by the United States Army Recruiting Service

Moxie was purposefully patriotic. Moxie phonograph records of World War I songs are now a very rare find.

This omnipresent Moxie Man poster, more than any other device, reminded folks to drink Moxie. It originally portrayed a young man in a stiff collar from which streamed a cravat bearing a letter "M" stickpin; and he really leaned toward you. Later, following fashion's dictate, the collar softened and sprouted points; and the old-fashioned stickpin disappeared. Still, the Moxie Man remained a well-known symbol of The Moxie Company. This mesmerizing character was probably the idea of Frank M. Archer, who became the great shaker and mover for the company. Legend has it that this Moxie Man was none other than Frank M. Archer, himself, not really a deity at all.

"Moxie," Dallas Mundy went on to say, "came in apothe-

"She took him to her parlor. She cooled him with her fan. She whispered in her Mother's ear: 'I love the Moxie Man.'"

cary-type bottles we used to put in our wooden refrigerator to chill against a block of sanitary Hygeia ice. The label was orange with gospel-black lettering. Moxie wasn't soda pop. Heaven forfend! Who, pray tell, would drink for pleasure? This pungent, tangy, fizzing, bubbly, wonderful stuff was tonic. In New England, carbonated beverages are still called that.

"But the biggest thrill of all was when the Moxiemobile came to town. There was something almighty grand about the rider in his hunter's red coat and his peaked cap. He was so much more dignified than that crazy 'Sunny Jim' who dressed up like a silly dude and ran around jumping over back-yard fences and handing out samples of a new breakfast cereal, called 'Force,' to mothers hanging up clothes back there or tending spaded-up patches of kitchen gardens where they grew 'sass' for the table—with enough left over to 'put up' for the winter.

"My own mother would have died before she'd be caught with store-bought packaged or canned goods in the house. When she recently saw that Campbell's Beans thing hanging on the wall of my living room, she blew her stack. 'Pop art, my foot!' she scolded. 'But that old Moxie bottle on the window sill sure catches

This title to a Moxie photographic tour lends credence to the legend. The Moxie Men figures in the background may very well have been Frank Archer himself.

the light real purty. Whatever happened to that little, tin Moxiemobile toy Mr. Perkins gave you years ago? My, didn't you think you were some punkins with that!'"

Although the various, full-size Moxie advertising vehicles were of vast importance, The Moxie Company's space ads in the media didn't take a back seat to anyone else's. Moxie was always alert to tie its ads in with current events, fads and even food. When the eclipse of the sun, in 1931, was due through Vermont, New

Simpson Spring still sells Moxie.

Hampshire, Maine and Massachusetts, the Boston *Post* of August 31st carried a banner headline announcing the phenomenon. That paper's front page also carried a three-column ad proclaiming that "Moxie Eclipses Everything!" The Simpson Spring, still a very active Moxie distributor, also had an ad on this page.

Long before Chevrolet thought of doing so, Moxie linked itself to hot dogs, that 1893 import from Germany which was becoming a very popular treat at baseball games and other outings. A contemporary of Nipper, the "His Master's Voice" mascot of the Victor Talking Machine Company; and Tige, the constant

Eating hot dogs and drinking Moxie.

companion of Buster Brown of children's shoes fame; was a
spotted, tail-wagging pup known as the Moxie Dog.

In an ad featuring Kid Moxie—a 7-ounce bottle of Moxie
recommended by none other than the Moxie Kid himself—was
this Moxie Dog carrying a "Hot Dog" sign in his mouth. Below,
the ad copy read: "Moxie and Hot Dogs just naturally go together.
Moxie makes you digest your food better and it's a mighty
satisfying drink with any lunch. Kid Moxie, the generous single-
size drink, is just the thing for picnics and roadside lunches." The
idea of advertising a soft drink as being good with things to eat may
have originated with Moxie at this time.

Capitalizing on the attraction of celebrity names, Moxie came
on with posters and ads in which not only Ed Wynn but also Jack
Donahue, George M. Cohan and Ann Pennington sponsored
Moxie. Later, Ted Williams went to bat for Moxie as well as Ted's
Root Beer. Ann Pennington, "The Girl With the Dimpled
Knees," was not the only heart-breaking hoofer who danced the
"Moxie Trot." This fast number was also a favorite of Irene Castle
who, with her husband, Vernon, made ballroom dancing respect-
able with their "Castle Walk," "Hesitation Waltz," and the
"Maxixe"—not to mention such gyrations as the "Texas Tommy"
and the "Grizzly Bear."

In 1921, The Moxie Company published sheet music for
"Moxie," a one-step, with music by Norman Leigh and lyrics by
Dennis J. Shea, which reiterated much that their earlier "singing

One of New England's Famous Sons

Clean, honest, intelligent, energetic, an American to the backbone, who has shared his brains, efforts and money with others to a greater extent than most any man living. His acquaintance and friendship is a possession to be proud of. He is a man of strong convictions, thinks and acts according to the dictates of his own fertile brain. One of the most versatile men living. Truly a man of achievements. And lest you forget, the following will refresh your memory:

BY F. M. ARCHER.

Running for Office
Governor's Son
Little Johnny Jones
Forty-Five Minutes from
    Broadway
George Washington, Jr.
Broadway Jones
Willow Tree
Three Faces East
Little Teacher
Seven Keys to Baldpate
Officer 666

Miracle Man
The Yankee Prince
Cohan's Revue
Fifty Miles from Boston
Yankee Doodle Dandy
Mary's a Grand Old Name
Royal Vagabond
Genius and the Crowd
Get-Rich-Quick-Wallingford
The Little Millionaire
The Talk of New York
The American Idea
The Man who owns Broadway
The Acquittal
Hello Broadway
Over There
Over Here
The Aviators
Going Up
So Long Mary
Popularity
Harrigan
When You Come Back
There Is a Whole World
    Waiting for You.

GEO. M. COHAN

George M. Cohan was a pall bearer at Frank Archer's funeral.

Buck Jones rides the Hollywood range for Moxie. His own white horse was named "Silver Buck."

This "Moxie" record belongs to George A. Blacker of Cheshire, Connecticut. It has the same lyrics and music as the "Moxie (one step) Song" that appeared as sheet music. The flip side has a fox trot (same melody but played at a slower tempo) by Raderman's Orchestra.

commercial" had to say about Moxie, but didn't continue the claim that it would "build up your nerve." The Moxie Company also published a "Moxie Fox Trot Song" with music by Eddie Fitzgerald and lyrics by the redoubtable Dennis J. Shea. Earlier, Moxie had produced a phonograph record of patriotic songs written to encourage young men to join the armed forces.

Large, metal Moxie signs were generously provided to Mom and Pop road stands. These hard-scrabble establishments sprang up like mushrooms with the advent of Henry Ford's "Tin Lizzie" and their folksy proprietors delighted in adding their own crudely lettered signs reading: "Mom's Home Made Pies, Pop on Ice." Hopefully, the "Pop" would include Moxie. Sometimes the durable Moxie signs—like their Coca Cola, Hires and Mail Pouch chewing tobacco contemporaries—wound up as serviceable roofs for outhouses.

Throughout this period, Moxie produced many advertising novelties, again handing out lollipops to the kids. Now, however, these goodies were no longer in the shape of The Moxie Candy Man's head. In a letter to the editor of the Maine *Sunday Telegram* of August 28, 1977, Bill Morrow of Poland Spring wrote: "I recall, in 1924, being at the Concord-Lexington, Mass. April 19th celebration parade, when the man on the Moxie Wagon passed out lollipops by the dozen, to get the kids used to the taste, I imagine. At any rate, these little suckers in the form of the Moxie Wagon with horse and driver, did just that for me and, through the years, I would guess I had my share of the trusty drink with the unforgettable flavor."

Other edible novelties included Moxie Candy in a little, yellow, metal box with red lettering—which sold for five cents; and Medicated Moxie Lozenges in a small, slide-out, cardboard box colored orange and black—"Give sweet sleep. Cure nervousness. Rest you if tired. One taken after exposure will prevent taking cold. Harmless in large quantities." For stores selling Moxie, there were fancy syrup dispensers for fountain use; and metal signs with cherry frames for bicycle stands at the curb outside.

An article in the *Western Collector* of July/August, 1970, claimed that the variety of novelties produced by Moxie was not as great as that for Coca Cola. This statement is subject to questioning inasmuch as nobody really knows just how many different items Moxie did produce over the years. Furthermore, to the cognoscenti, Moxie items are the creme de la creme of soda pop collectibles. "I collect Moxie items became their quality is better than Coke's," says Peter Travera, an astute Connecticut dealer. "Also, they are a superior investment."

Among the multitude of things which have turned up and been collected that weren't novelty items, but should be mentioned, are the Moxie bottles—and there is a considerable quantity of these, from the early Baltimore Loop Seal type, invented by William Painter, through a number of different designs. The Baltimore Loop Seal, used by Moxie from about 1890 until 1905,

Moxie

Words by DENNIS J. SHEA

Music by NORMAN LEIGH

was expendable and consisted of a cloth-covered rubber disc that was fitted into a groove inside the mouth of the bottle. It was tightened by the pressure of the bottle's contents. A small attached metal ring was used to remove the seal.

The very common high-shouldered Moxie bottle—shown in early advertisements which stated that Moxie came only in the 26-ounce size—later appeared in a 16-ounce and a Kid Moxie 7-ounce size. These bottles had MOXIE embossed on their shoulders. A few of them may still be in use by some New England bottlers

with old-style equipment, to whom these old bottles are still being returned for refilling—in spite of the fact that a single 7-ounce Moxie bottle of this type can bring more on the collectors' market than the bottler may be asking for a case of them full of Moxie, not to mention the value of the old wooden case itself.

Moxie mugs and glasses are still to be found. Ones with "Licensed only for serving Moxie" embossed on them are particularly desirable. If you should find one with a mark near the bottom, indicating the level to which the syrup should come before

The western
COLLECTOR

50¢

VOLUME VIII   NUMBERS 7 & 8   JULY/AUGUST 1970

MOXIE
®

DISTINCTLY DIFFERENT!

DRINK
MOXIE

Drink
MOXIE

Bill Gaylord reports on
Moxie, from its inception
in 1884 to its present
operation. Once a bigger
seller than Coca Cola,
Moxie now offers collectors
a variety of fascinating and
very collectible advertiques.

Pioneer for Today's Collector

WESTERN COLLECTOR IS THE OFFICIAL VOICE OF THE FEDERATION OF HISTORICAL BOTTLE CLUBS.

Cover reproduced by permission of The Antiques Journal, *Dubuque, Iowa.*

the fizz water is added, you have discovered a rare collectible indeed. Some Moxie glasses were crystal and were distributed for Moxie VIP use. Glasses with Moxie appearing on a red, frosted band were also made.

On the earlier mugs and glasses, the raised name had a simple "X" whereas later ones sported the familiar "X" with a long, looping crossbar. Some embossments had loops from the letters "M" and "E." "I sure like that Moxie X," one old-timer remarked. "Sort of marks the spot, so to speak. I never learned how to write, but I made out pretty good anyhow just makin' my own X."

This Moxie logotype, which has appeared in various designs on bottles, mugs, glasses and wooden cases was used (and still is) on all Moxie stationery, advertisements, publications, products and novelties with rare exception. If you see it on something, you can be sure it's a genuine product. The various Moxie companies and the present Moxie Industries have always watched over this logotype with proprietary zeal.

Tiffany Moxie lampshades are a collector's dream. Even a reproduction at $125 would be a bargain. One of these shades was shown hanging over a pool table in the popular movie "Goodbye Columbus." Other Moxie novelties include yardsticks of unusual shape—square rather than flat, so that they may also be used as walking sticks; valentines; all sorts of trays—some of glass with imprinting on the underside and having metal rims and handles; countless cardboard fans—with pictures on them of silent movie queens, cowboys, the Moxie Man, etc.; celluloid, folding "ivory" fans—with Moxie perforated in the blades; stand-up wooden Moxie Butlers and Moxie Maids; dishes of all sorts—with pictures of the Moxie Man or a Moxie Girl on them; variously designed bottle openers—some serving also as stoppers; metal and cardboard finger-spin tops; stickpins; lavaliers; cigars; etc. etc. etc.

Collectors also look for Moxie paper goods such as three- and six-pack cardboard totes, bags and the like, the variety of which boggles the mind. The lettering on many Moxie collectibles will inform you that they were designed and patented by Frank M. Archer.

Occasionally, wire bottle openers can be found with Moxie on one side and Puroxia on the other. Similarly designed Moxie and Puroxia signs often appeared side by side. Puroxia was a brand of ginger ale marketed by The Moxie Company, which also produced

Fairly modern Moxie six-packs. The one in the middle has no bottom. It is a "Top Grip" (Trademark of J. B. Slevin Co. Inc.) device. The crown caps on the bottles are pushed up through—and thus caught under—the holes in the top of the carton. These containers are for 10-oz bottles, not the 7-oz bottles shown in this photo.

ginger ale under the Moxie name. One collector of Moxiana was lucky enough to discover a cache of unused, gold-colored, Crown-type, Moxie Ginger Ale bottle caps. It is rumored that the Moxie Company may have attempted the sale of carbonated beverages with still more flavors.

Moxie was a forerunner in the diet drink market, being one of the first soft-drink manufacturers to create and produce a sugar-free concentrate bearing its own name. In the late 1960s, The Moxie Company was producing approximately forty percent of its total product in the form of Diet Moxie.

Ever aware of the youth market, Moxie dubbed its 7-oz. bottle the Kid Moxie size. Family, for the 26-oz. and Club, for the 16-oz. were common size designations.

The Moxie Maid and Moxie Butler were designed to serve as standing ash trays.

It has been reported that, in the early 1920s, with the cost of sugar rising, Moxie decided to reduce its advertising budget and use the money to buy sugar. On the other hand, some knowledgeable old-timers claim that Moxie began selling sugar to Canadian firms during this period. Whatever the case, Moxie advertising did decline; and so did its sales. Franchise holders began dropping Moxie and switching to Coca Cola and other brands more vigorously promoted.

According to *Business Week* of May 20, 1967, Moxie has been going "down the drain" since the Depression of the 1930s, during which the company decided to stop its national advertising and confine its sales efforts to New England and nearby states. Outselling Coca Cola in 1920, Moxie had reached a peak of twenty-five million cases in 1925, and had a distribution in thirty-five states. In 1927, the company was reorganized as a corporation with

Moxie-flavored lollipops were given to children to accustom them to the taste.

Predecessor of today's disposable cardboard six-pack container, this Moxie Carrying Bag had "a hundred later uses."

public stock. Eventually, the Moxie corporation was held by some 1700 to 1800 shareholders, approximately a million shares having been issued.

Although Moxie doubtlessly cut back on much of its advertising, it didn't neglect radio. Schedules of when and where Moxie used this medium may have long since been lost during management shuffles, but at least one record remains—a phonograph record belonging to Nick "Moxie Bananas" Zaffiro, one of the early Moxiemobile drivers. This 78-rpm disc was produced by the Kasper-Gordon Studios, Inc. at 140 Boylston Street, Boston, Massachusetts, and contains eight 55-second segments. On one side are four musical programs; and on the other, four dramatic presentations. The label on this record is not dated, but there can be no doubt that it was made soon after the United States entered World War II.

A four-cylinder Buick Moxiemobile in a Massachusetts cavalcade with The Moxie Company's Pureoxia ginger ale. The Moxiemobiles were always magnets for kids.

Each of the musical segments begins with, "What this country needs is plenty of Moxie." This was a slogan much used by The Moxie Company. A lapel button, depicting Uncle Sam's hat and bearing this slogan, turned up in a collection of Moxie items distributed during World War I.

The first musical segment continues with: "The All American Victory Quartet. I'm North; I'm South; I'm East; I'm West. And

we'll sing you a song about...about...Gosh, about what?"...
"C'mon, boys, sing something. You're on the air."...."But we
don't know what to sing; what'll we do?"..."You need Moxie,
boys. Here, drink this" (sounds of Moxie being poured)...
"That's just what we needed...C'mon, boys, we'll sing them the
Moxie Song:

"The Army, the Navy, the Air Corps and Marines; they've
got Moxie.

And you folks at home building all our war machines; you'll
need Moxie.

It's cooling and refreshing; it's sure to give you pep;

And when you march along with Moxie, you'll be right in
step.

So buy it and try it if you want victory, you'll need Moxie."

The three musical segments which follow this involve scenes
at the Bar-Nothin' Ranch, a USO dance, and a bagpipers' get-
together. Each program ends with the Moxie Song. No matter how
corny this Moxie singing commercial may seem today, it was well
attuned to the tastes of millions of radio listeners who loved "Rosie
the Riveter," "Don't Sit Under the Apple Tree," and "In der
Fuhrer's Face."

Each of the four dramatic segments starts the same way. A
politician-type voice shouts: "And, ladies and gentlemen, what
this country needs is plenty of Moxie." After which someone in the
audience whispers to someone else: "Say, Mister, what's this
Moxie everyone's talking about?"—and is answered: "What's
Moxie? Just listen!" One of the programs then follows with:

"John Smith, you lay um head on block. Indian go chop chop.
John Smith lose head. Unh!"...."No, no, Big Chief; don't kill um
John Smith. Me, Pocahontas, love paleface."...."Too bad, me,
Big Chief, no like paleface son-in-law."...."Oh, my poor Indian
heart, she go broke. Oh, oh..." Stage whisper: "Try Moxie. Here,
give him this." (sound of Moxie being poured). "Wait, wait, Big
Chief. Drink paleface magic water, Moxie."...."Moxie, Unh!
...Ah! Moxie good!"...."Then you no kill um John Smith?"
..."Kill um? No; we make paleface big chief; we sing 'For he's a
jolly good fellow; for he's a...'"

Announcer: "No matter what your favorite drink has been,
switch to Moxie and see for yourself what wonderful refreshment
there is in this pure, wholesome drink with a flavor of woodland
herbs. Get Moxie today!"

46

Each dramatic program ends with a similar pitch for Moxie. The other three such segments have to do with a defense plant bottleneck, the launching of a battleship—the *Miami Beach*—and Simon Legree chasing Lisa. Each situation is, of course, relieved by a bottle of Moxie.

Recently, in commercials during Red Sox games being broadcast from Fenway Park in Boston, Ted Williams could be heard extolling the virtues of Moxie.

During Moxie's slump, many management changes were tried; but nothing seemed to help. Even a sortie into the potato-chip business failed to give Moxie the shot in the arm it so sorely needed. Two separately incorporated Moxie organizations were attempted. The Moxie Company, incorporated in Massachusetts (formerly a Maine corporation) with F. E. Thompson as president and F. M. Archer as vice president, was established with offices in Boston as exclusive manufacturer and distributor of Moxie in New England. This company retained ownership of the Moxie trademark and formula. The Moxie Company of America, incorporated in Delaware with F. M. Archer as president and his son as treasurer, was established with offices in Boston and New York as exclusive licensee for the United States (except New England) and for all foreign countries.

The converted brewery in Roxbury was a showplace in which the Moxie Companies took considerable pride. A pioneer industrial film tour, "Frank Archer Invites You to Visit Moxieland," was produced there. At least one copy of this filmstrip still exists. It also belongs to Nicholas Zaffiro of Revere, Massachusetts.

By the summer of 1962, The Moxie Company had long since located in Needham Heights, Massachusetts, near Boston. At this time, Orville Purdy (a nephew of Frank Archer) was General Manager. He cheerfully related that, "The Moxie business is still going strong, although sales are mostly confined to New England." In 1966, the company sold only about 500,000 cases, grossing some $200,000.

Early in 1967, a Connecticut lawyer by the name of Mcgregor Kilpatrick and two of his partners became members of Moxie's board of directors. Kilpatrick had a head for business, having been a vice president with Marketing Inc. where he was instrumental in putting Silly Putty into the hands of millions of American children. Kilpatrick put Moxie's potato-chip business to rest and scouted for someone to manage Moxie's tonic enterprise. He found

MOXIELAND
HEATH, PARKER AND BICKFORD STS.
BOSTON (ROXBURY DIST.) MASS.

James C. Wickersham, a former top official with McCann-Erickson, the advertising agency. Wickersham had handled the Coca Cola account and had had twelve years experience in plant-feeding, vending, and soft-drink business in Philadelphia.

Later in the year, Moxie bought the National NuGrape Company of Atlanta, Georgia, and combined the two firms—setting up headquarters in Doraville, Georgia, in 1968, as the Moxie-Monarch-NuGrape Company. Wickersham was able to assemble over a quarter of a million dollars, including some of his own funds. His plan was to increase the number of Moxie bottlers beyond the then three dozen or so, with more in New England. He would then build a regional marketing and advertising campaign to spread out over the whole country.

What bothered Wickersham considerably was Moxie's taste, which he felt was too much like medicine. He believed that folks would now like something sweeter. "We want to get rid of that bitter after-taste," he said, "and make Moxie more attractive to a

A few frames from the Moxieland film strip.

greater number of people. But we still want it to be distinctively Moxie." Unfortunately, the new Moxie didn't turn out to be all that distinctive. The drink, that had been heavy and tangy, was rebalanced to give it a contemporary taste aimed at the youth market. To some, Moxie, in its new dimpled bottles, was as sweet as the dimpled Shirley Temple—altogether too sweet to bear the name of Moxie. Reportedly, it tasted like no more than a carbonated fruit punch.

Our visitors see trucks leaving for all points of the compass,

Ford Model A "Tudor" sedans had long since replaced the open Buick Moxie autos.

and the famous horsemobiles starting on parade to remind us of the world's finest drink, MOXIE.

In this unusual photograph, showing six Moxie horsemobiles together, is a rare shot of the 6-cylinder Buick—followed by the Rolls-Royce and four LaSalles.

50

The First Horsemobile,

This contraption, with a horse in the sidecar, is sometimes called the Moxiecycle.

and that familiar saying, "He's got plenty of MOXIE."

Like Harold Lloyd hanging onto the clock hand in "Safety Last."

"The (MOXIE) Kid" The Charlie Chaplin film advertised on marquee in the background is the 1936 hit, "Modern Times."

No "block of sanitary Hygeia ice" but plenty of Moxie.

This, perhaps, is where Wickersham erred in his thinking. Most of his advertising was also to be "aimed straight at the youth market." "We want to make the product contemporary," he said, "but we don't want to lose our older customers." But straddling a generation or two may have been more of a stretch than Mr. Wickersham contemplated. To begin with, his advertising budget was to be modest. "After all," he said, "we don't have to spend millions of dollars launching a new name...what appealed to me about Moxie is the name, and I'm excited about the possibility of rebuilding something that has been abused over the last thirty years. We have a full skeleton; our job is to put some meat on its bones." He then added, somewhat cryptically: "What's more, there is a whole lot of humor in the whole situation."

Funny bones aside, although his youth market was familiar enough with the word "moxie" (without perhaps ever knowing there had once been a popular drink by that name), the new flavor of Moxie didn't reflect the macho meaning that the words held for the kids. The new Moxie should have had more zap, more pizazz!

Newsweek of November 10, 1969, reported that The Moxie Company was located in Atlanta, Georgia; that James C. Wickersham was board chairman and Frank A. Armstrong (also from McCann-Erickson's Coca Cola account) was president.

On November 24, 1969, Mr. Armstrong wrote: "Yes, we are expanding MOXIE! We had twenty-six bottlers in the New England area. Now bottlers have been added in such markets as Asbury Park, New Jersey; Newark, New Jersey; Gadsden, Alabama; Franklin, Louisiana; Minneapolis, Minnesota; Alaska; and Albany, New York. A total of some twenty new bottlers in the last twelve months...It (Moxie) is completely different from the old...but palatable and some say delicious."

By the late 1970s, Frank Armstrong had become President of Moxie Industries in Atlanta, a consolidation of some seven companies—including Moxie International, and ranging in products from bubble gum to ice cream boosters. The Monarch Company in the Moxie Industries complex had, by 1977, become the leading brand franchiser of soft drinks, with over 1,000 bottlers. Among their brands were: NuGrape, Grapette, Suncrest (various flavors), Kist, Nesbitts, Masons Root Beer, Dr. Wells (to compete with Dr. Pepper), lemon-orange Kickapoo Joy Juice... and Moxie.

When Frank Armstrong came to the Company, Moxie had

Frank Armstrong, President, The Moxie Company; Lionel H. Stutz, President, National NuGrape Company; Sam Dixon, Chairman, and George Dixon, President, Monarch Citrus Products Company, are shown with products of the combined companies.

been its sole brand. On October 5, 1978, Armstrong's office reported that Moxie now contributed "a very, very small portion of our total sales figures. Moxie, despite marketing efforts, remained a New Englander's beverage, it remains in New England now, much to the dismay of transplanted New Englanders living in other sections of the country."

But why had Moxie become low man on Monarch's soda pop poll? And how was it faring in New England, that traditional bastion of loyal Moxie Drinkers? Well, Yankees—being the sort of people they are—were not about to be switched into accepting an interloper flying under false colors. The new and "completely different" drink may have been "palatable and some say delicious" but it wasn't Moxie!

On July 21, 1980, Frank Armstrong (now Chairman of the Board of Moxie Industries) wrote: "We tried to change Moxie to a more palatable drink years ago and our sales in New England dropped about fifty percent until we put the old drink back (the current drink)." Inasmuch as the "completely different" Moxie

The "GREAT NEW TASTE" turned out to be a disappointment to older Moxie drinkers.

The dimpled Moxie bottle of the 1960s is now a collector's item.

was short-lived, the 10-ounce dimpled bottles in which it was marketed are now somewhat hard-to-come-by collectibles. When Moxie Industries put the old drink back, they put it in still another shape of bottle—and in cans—and called it Old Fashion Moxie.

The "old drink" had made its last previous appearance when the Moxie Company was still in its Needham Heights, Massachusetts plant. The old-style, high-shouldered bottles were still being used—in both the 7-ounch and the 1-pint, 10-ounce sizes—but the familiar orange-with-black-lettering paper labels had been re-

New and old Moxie bottles atop a marble counter in Frank Anicetti's store in Lisbon Falls, Maine. The glasses are old; the tray is new.

Old Moxie Nerve Food bottle.

Embossed Moxie glass

placed by enamel labels which could withstand sterilizing when bottles were returned for refilling. Any embossed Moxie bottle still bearing its paper label in good condition is a rare find.

The paper label on the bottle at the left bears a July 7, 1914 date. Center bottles have enamel labels.

To assure customers that the drink was the same, the new labels contained the word "Original." Because, after 1960, sassafras was banned from use, the Moxie subsequently produced wasn't quite as original as it might have been. The main ingredient, however, was still in it. The backs of the enamel-labeled bottles read: "MOXIE is a wholesome carbonated beverage made from the extracts of gentian root and other natural flavors, cane sugar and caramel color."

The Moxie Company of Boston placed great value on its trademark, its labels and even the particular shape of the original Moxie bottle—dating back to when Moxie Nerve Food was produced. Chapter 5, "Of Bottles and Battles," tells about the lengths to which the Moxie Company went to protect itself against imitation, intimation, implication, or what have you.

CHAPTER 4

"Avoir du Chien"

"Moxie" has been referred to as a household word. This, it may be; but it is much more. It now has an esteemed status upon the high seas. On June 25, 1980, at 8:12 a.m., Philip Saltonstall Weld, in a trimaran, crossed the finish line at Newport, Rhode Island, to become the first American to win the prestigious Observer Singlehanded Transatlantic Race (OSTAR). Moxie enough, it took, even to complete this 3000-mile solo race; but Phil, for the greater glory of Gloucester, Massachusetts, bettered the previous record by more than 2½ days. Also, at sixty-five, he was the senior of eighty-eight contestants, many of whom were but half his age. According to *Yachting* magazine: "This was, without a doubt, the most popular victory by one man in the history of yacht racing."

Weld claimed that his voyage had not been difficult. . . that he was not "a great seaman" but simply an "assiduous" one. When pressed for details, however, he admitted that he had averaged less than five hours of sleep at night and that—upon eventually learning that the winning margin he had so assiduously piled up had deteriorated during some light winds—he had then taken the only "imprudent" action of the crossing and, like a gaunt ghost, had driven his boat at speeds topping twenty knots through fog during the last week in a successful attempt to protect his lead. The name of his creditable craft? The "Moxie."

But how did Sailor Weld, the "Gloucester Ghost," happen to christen his boat "Moxie?" Was it because he was sponsored by Moxie Industries? Not so! Nevertheless, Phil is in favor of sponsorship. "It's the only way I can see," says he, "that most of the youthful and impecunious will be able to afford good boats for

Aboard his trimaran, "Moxie," Phil Weld crosses the finish line in record time.
Wide World Photos

this sort of racing. If it works for golf and tennis, why not for sailing too? Mind you, there are French vintners willing to pay thousands for the right to put their product name upon an entry's transom."

The well-heeled Mr. Weld doesn't really need a sponsor. Still, being without one bothers him. "It makes me feel like the poor little rich kid," he says, "with no one on the block to play with." So, while sailing from England to Bermuda, in May, 1978, with Allerton "Ats" Cushman aboard, Phil turned to his companion and shouted into the wind: "Help me! Come up with a good name for a mock sponsor to put on my next boat."

While doing his three-hour trick at the helm, Ats pondered the problem. "Mock sponsor?" he kept asking himself, "Mock?...mock?...mock?"

"Moxie!" he cried, when Phil returned to the deck, "That's it! Let's recreate the company."

"Issue stock!" Phil joined in, "Big PR drive! Souvenirs! Fun!"

But research soon revealed that Moxie was far from defunct. Moxie Industries was flourishing in Georgia. "When I phone the Moxie office in Atlanta," an understandably exasperated Phil told friends, "I can never get the president even to speak to me. He apparently thinks I'm some kind of a wild man."

Nevertheless, President Frank Armstrong's secretary did tell Phil that there'd be no objection to his naming his boat "Moxie." He was even promised a bottle of Moxie for the launching. He never received the bottle; but the names "Moxie" and "Phil Weld" were thenceforth wedded for posterity. "Moxie," says Phil, "comes through unmistakably on voice radio; at least it does in Maine waters."

Setting sail for Europe prior to the OSTAR, the "Moxie" carried a ream of leaflets with the message from the label of an old BEVERAGE MOXIE NERVE FOOD bottle Phil had seen reproduced in the June, 1979, issue of *Yankee* magazine. It is the same one that begins Chapter 1 of this book. Phil distributed these leaflets in France, Britain and Newport.

In France, Phil was interviewed by a major radio network regarding the implications of the name of his boat. "From the only bottle of Moxie in the Common Market—that we freighted over," says Phil, "I served swallows to the French press, who responded with grimaces for the TV cameraman, and wrote about it in the national press."

"Avoir du chien!" exclaimed one gallant Gaul—which expression is, of course, an excellent translation of the American word "moxie" into French.

Never before had a product for which a boat had been named

received so much print and air space. The New York *Times, Sports Illustrated,* the Boston *Globe,* the Washington *Post,* the yachting journals of six nations—to name only a few—repeated the Moxie legend after that OSTAR victory.

Undaunted by the seeming indifference of Moxie Industries toward their hero, some of the Weld children and grandchildren turned the other cheek and greeted the "Wild Man" at dockside with a banner inscribed: "Moxie Quenches Your Thirst."

Phil Weld's son-in-law, Mac Bell, who runs The Glass Sailboat, a small department store in Gloucester, had orange T-shirts printed with the "Moxie" sailing on the chest and that old Moxie label reproduced on the back. Mac phoned Moxie Industries in Atlanta and chided the firm for not being at Newport to greet Phil with fanfare and pennants flying. This phone call brought a letter from a vice president in charge of marketing announcing that a package would be arriving via UPS. Inside, Phil found "a styrofoam clock painted like wood, a golf cap, a belt buckle, a shoulder patch and a ball point pen."

What's Phil Weld's own definition of "moxie?" "Well," he says, "I guess it goes back to those old Horatio Alger books. Remember their theme, 'Pluck in Adversity?' Then there was that 1923 Damon Runyon short story in which he wrote that a prize fighter had 'showed he had lots of moxie' when he picked himself up off the floor to go on to win. Maybe that's the sort of moxie they say I had when I imprudently raced through the fog to win in the OSTAR."

According to *The American Thesaurus of Slang,* "moxie" means "confidence, impudence, audacity, impertinent assurance, fighting spirit," and "skill as a baseball player." *Webster's* adds that the word is slang for "energy, pep, life, courage, nerve, stamina, backbone," and "guts;" and that it comes from "'Moxie,' a trademark for a soft drink." *The New Random House Dictionary of the English Language* defines it as "Slang 1. vigor, verve, pep. 2. courage, and aggressiveness, nerve. (formerly trademark (name of a soft drink))." The 1979 edition of *Webster's New Collegiate Dictionary* gives the following unusual use of the word by G.S. Perry: "Streetcars with so much moxie, they can run out from under you."

Random House's use of the word "formerly" is unfortunate. Moxie with an upper-case "M" is still very much the copyrighted trademark of the Moxie organization and remains the oldest name

No. 159066

The United States of America

To All To Whom These PRESENTS Shall Come:

This is to Certify That by the records of the UNITED STATES PATENT OFFICE it appears that THE MOXIE COMPANY, of Portland, Maine, and Boston, Massachusetts, a corporation organized under the laws of the State of Maine,

did, on the 26th day of March, 1923 , duly file in said Office an application for REGISTRATION of a certain

TRADE-MARK

shown in the drawing for the goods specified in the statement, copies of which drawing and statement are hereto annexed, and duly complied with the requirements of the law in such case made and provided, and with the regulations prescribed by the COMMISSIONER OF PATENTS.

And, upon due examination, it appearing that the said applicant is entitled to have said TRADE-MARK registered under the law, the said TRADE-MARK has been duly REGISTERED this day in the UNITED STATES PATENT OFFICE, to

The Moxie Company, its successors or assigns.

This certificate shall remain in force for TWENTY YEARS, unless sooner terminated by law.

In Testimony Whereof I have hereunto set my hand and caused the seal of the PATENT OFFICE to be affixed, at the City of Washington, this ninth day of September, in the year of our Lord one thousand nine hundred and twenty-four, and of the Independence of the United States the one hundred and forty-ninth.

Karl Finn

Acting Commissioner of Patents.

in the soft-drink industry. Perhaps moxie with a lower-case "m" has passed into the public domain. Nevertheless, the use of the

63

UNITED STATES PATENT OFFICE.

THE MOXIE COMPANY, OF PORTLAND, MAINE, AND BOSTON, MASSACHUSETTS

ACT OF FEBRUARY 20, 1905.

Application filed March 26, 1923.   Serial No. 178,054.

STATEMENT.

the Commissioner of Patents:

he Moxie Company, a corporation y organized under the laws of the e of Maine, and located in the City ortland, county of Cumberland, in State, and doing business at 61-71 erhill Street, Boston, Massachu-s, has adopted and used the trade-k shown in the accompanying ving, for a NONALCOHOLIC, LTLESS CARBONATED BEV-GE AND SIRUP FOR MAK- THE SAME, in Class 45, Bever-, nonalcoholic, and presents here-five specimens showing the trade-k as actually used by applicant the goods, and requests that the be registered in the United States nt Office in accordance with the f February 20, 1905, as amended.

e trade-mark has been continu-y used and applied to said goods by pplicant and its predecessors from m title was derived since the year and such use has been exclusive. applicant is the owner of trade-

mark registrations No. 12,565 A. Thompson and No. 62,295 to Moxie Nerve Food Company of 1 England.

The trade-mark is usually app or affixed to the goods by pla thereon a printed label on which trade-mark is shown.

Applicant hereby appoints Ol Mitchell, Everett D. Chadwick Everett E. Kent, constituting the f of Mitchell, Chadwick & Kent, (F No. 8481), of 99 State Street, Bost Massachusetts, its attorneys, to pr cute this application for registrat with full powers of substitution revocation, to make alterations amendments therein, to receive certificate of registration and to tra act all business in the Patent Of connected therewith.

THE MOXIE COMPANY,

By FRANK M. ARCHER

Vice-President.

word (type case notwithstanding) should not be adopted for commercial purposes, nor should it be claimed by any other organization as its own.

What moxie means to young and old was reiterated in a 1970s magazine article, "Moxie Bridges the (generation) Gap":

> Yesterday I asked a man what moxie means. "Smarts," he said. "A guy who's got moxie is a guy who's got his smarts." Another man assured me that it refers especially to nerve, smart-alecky nerve, with enough behind it to back it up. A third came up with an excellent synonym: "chutzpah." "They're all wrong," an old-timer interrupted, "Moxie means when a pitcher's got plenty on the ball. . . and, no, I never heard of that American wha-cha-ma-call-it of slang." "Moxie?" a teen'age girl smiled, then performed a pirouette. "Look me over Daddy-O; I've got it! I'm wearing it! They didn't have to put it in the dictionary; everybody knows what moxie means."
>
> The young lady had said not only that she had moxie, but that she was wearing it. Maybe she meant her Moxees? But they were probably named that because they're moccasin-type shoes. The mystery was still bugging me when I opened the morning paper and saw an ad for a Moxie Party being given by a local smarte shoppe every Tuesday afternoon.
>
> "What's a Moxie Party?" I asked the clerk who answered the phone.
>
> "Well," she replied, "we simply put a lot of stuff out on the counters and the kids come in and pick out what they want. They put it together as they please."
>
> "Just like that? All mixed up? That's moxie?"
>
> "If you don't know what moxie means, look it up in the dictionary. If you want to know how the kids are making with moxie, look in *Seventeen*; look in *Vogue*; look in *Mademoiselle*."
>
> The only other connection I'd ever seen between moxie and clothes was a line that appeared in *Fortnight* a long while ago: "Only in the British Empire do males have the moxie to regularly wear shorts in mixed company." Now, it seemed, the word also had to do with the way females dressed.
>
> On my lunch hour I browsed through some ladies' rags—magazines, that is. I found a lot of emphasis on the "put-together" look, but where was the tie-in to moxie? Back at the office, I glanced at the younger female-type employees, more than glanced at them. I made a close study of their hemlines, the color and design of what they were wearing, paid closest attention to the more appealing put-together girls. One well-tanned brunette with shoulder-length

hair—the one I'd seen tooling to work in her Corvette—stood out clothes-wise and otherwise from the rest.

"Moxie fashions?" she smiled, "Hold the fort! I think what you're looking for is in the powder room."

She brought me back the June, 1969, issue of *Mademoiselle.* On the cover beside the pretty face of a straight-haired blonde was "How To Put Yourself Together The Way A Model Does." On page sixteen, "Our Cover" told me that the girl was Jeanne Branton, and that she was one of the models "moxie-ing" around in the magazine. Hah! This is something girls *do*? Moxie can also be a verb?

Back to the contents page, under "Fashion," I discovered that pages 98 through 107 contained an article "How To Put Yourself Together With A Model's Moxie." This is where *Mademoiselle* told it like it is. Fashionwise, "moxie" was their next word. It meant, the magazine said, brio, guts, bravura. Everybody is supposed to have it to some extent. Allegedly, Barbra Streisand has it, *is* it. The article went on to explain what "moxie" means to fashion, and that this issue was full of it. (But *Mademoiselle* was too full of "moxie" to suit The Moxie Company. According to *Mademoiselle's* public relations director: "We had a little trouble with The Moxie Company about the use of this term.")

As Jimmy Durante would say (and who relates better with youngsters?), "Them's the conditions what prevails" in the semantics of moxie. This is one happy instance where the younger generation has accepted something from us over-thirties.

Moxie fashions were highlighted in a promotional exhibit in Dayton's Department Stores in the late 1960s. Chain-belted mannikins in miniskirts and blown-up photos of teenagers wearing "Chain Gang Shirts" appeared in window displays that brought thousands of customers to all Dayton's stores to try Moxie and buy Dayton's merchandise. Moxie was featured as the "in-drink" and, in just one evening, "College Night," 9,000 youngsters paid for and downed more than 12,000 bottles of Moxie and loved it. Three thousand cases of Moxie were sold in the first sixteen days of the month-long August Moxie Party.

In *Printers' Ink* for July 31, 1959, I found the following:

An ad man of our acquaintance was guzzling a bottle of Pepsi when his nine-year-old sauntered in to

MOXIE in key window locations

- Much of Dayton's valuable high-traffic window space was devoted to MOXIE in key locations.

- MOXIE was portrayed as the "in-drink" ... which it proved to be.

- These window displays brought thousands of customers to all Dayton's stores to try MOXIE and buy Dayton's merchandise.

inquire petulantly, "Why don't we have Moxie like other people?" Our friend recalled drinking Moxie (a bitter-tasting carbonated beverage) in his own youth, but not having heard a thing about it in thirty-five years, he shot some questions at his son, who informed him: "Everybody knows Moxie. It's in *Mad.*"

Mad, as many of us have been forced to learn, is a magazine quite what its name suggests, and it

delights in spoofing advertising ("See the difference color TV makes with RGA victim; clear heads agree that Culvert's D.T.'s are better.") and about anything else it can think of. Consulting his son's staggering collection of back issues, our ad man found at least twenty-nine allusions to Moxie sneaked in to the magazine's typically mad article illustrations. Was this horseplay actually reviving demand for the product? Our friend's curiosity made us curious too.

We started by calling the Moxie Co. in Needham, Massachusetts, where Orville Purdy, vice-president, let us know that things have never been better for the firm. We learned that Moxie...after seventy-five years of distribution confined (mostly) to the New England states, just recently expanded into Pennsylvania and California. In addition, Purdy told us, last year the company finally brought out a second product—Ted's Root Beer which, in a neat tie-in, features baseball player Ted Williams in its ads. Ted's (with distribution in Massachusetts and Maine) is reportedly already doing well, but Moxie is still the company's pride and joy. By last year, Moxie sales were double the 1952 level and, according to Purdy, "this year's sales are running eighteen per cent higher than last year's."

We asked Purdy if he knew what *Mad* was up to. "Well," he said, "they called to ask permission to reprint our logo and we gave it to them, but as far as a correlation between our sales and *Mad* is concerned, I wouldn't know."

Next I called Albert B. Feldstein, editor of *Mad*. He was inclined to think that his magazine, which started running the word moxie in December, 1958, might have had just a wee bit to do with the drink's eighteen per cent sales rise. "The whole business," he told me, "is something of an experiment. While we have never sold advertising space, we may in the future, although we won't solicit it, but let the advertisers discover us. We want to be prepared to show that *Mad* is read with tremendous depth, and that an ad, written in the *Mad* vernacular, would do very well for an advertiser, and Moxie sure proves it.

"You see," Feldstein explained, "we never made Moxie obvious by mentioning it in an article. We also never ran a satirical ad for it like we sometimes do for other products. We just stuck the Moxie logo in with the regular illustrations for articles and waited to see what happened.

"Ever since we started printing the word 'Moxie' inconspiciously, hundreds of letters have

come in about it," said Feldstein, adding that he would send a batch over for us to look through. The

letters arrived in bulk, and we had to admit *Mad* readers certainly are noticing Moxie. Most of the letters request enlightenment. For example: "Who is this Moxie? Your tailor?" Others have it all figured out, like the reader who writes: "Maybe the appearance of Moxie all over the place in your last issue is your idea of advertising by subliminal projection. Well—it doesn't work. I didn't even notice it."

A generation later, Jerry De Fuccio, associate editor at *Mad*, said that, when parents now visit *Mad* with their kids, these "old folks" show off their knowledge of *Mad* lore by dropping the name Moxie.

In her autobiography, *On Reflection*, Helen Hayes—harking back to when she was playing in Mary Roberts Rinehart's "Babs"—tells about the time she was walking on Boston Common with Mary's son, Alan. When Alan asked Helen to go to Peru with him, replied Helen: "I'm dying of thirst, Alan. May I have some Moxie?" The accomplished Miss Hayes thus missed an opportunity for a perfect put-down. She should have rebuffed Alan's proposition about Peru by telling him that he was full of Peruna.

In the summer of 1967, a nostalgic story in a popular men's magazine started off with: "When it came to girls, a guy could move in with a lot of moxie." Having moxie, it turned out, meant that you could cut the mustard.

Drawing courtesy of Mrs. Walt Kelly

As reported in *Time* on August 22, 1969, Ralph Salerno, the New York City Police Department's chief Mafia expert until his retirement in 1967, said (concerning the Mafia's leadership): "It's the three Ms—Moxie, muscle and money."

In the Sunday comics of June 8, 1969, Beauregarde, the dog, in Walt Kelly's Pogo strip exclaimed: "AFRAID!? Aha! Sully not the escutheon of the NOBLE DOG whose age-old courage is rife with unmottled MOXIE!" Walt had previously used the word in several of his daily strips.

In a November, 1969 issue of *Life*, the first word in a short article under a two-page photograph of the Kennedy clan is "moxie." The piece, titled "The Father of the Kennedys," begins: "'Moxie' was one of his favorite words, as it is for any old Irisher, and Joe Kennedy used it often to tell his four sons just what it was the world needed more of. Enough Moxie he had to make his way all the way up from East Boston, the Irish ghetto. ..."

In 1979, a newspaper item about a woman who decided not to tell her young daughter that she was dying of an incurable disease, quoted the woman as saying: "So it required a lot of...I guess you'd say acting, a lot of moxie. Determination." In the classified section of the same paper was a help-wanted ad offering a retail management trainee position to anyone who was "not afraid of long hours on occasion and/or the moxie to know when to mop the floors or make out the payroll."

In Judith Krantz's recent best seller, *Scruples*, she says: "No moxie; that's your trouble."

Today, "moxie" is spoken a lot on TV. Millions hear the word used to exemplify its many nuances. On "Police Story," Dennis Weaver, in talking to a convict, says: "You've got enough moxie to know." In "All in the Family," Archie Bunker asks George Jefferson: "Isn't there something in soul food that gives you a lot of moxie?" And, for the folks who might not know that Moxie is also a drink, a rerun of "The Honeymooners" has Art Carney asking Jackie Gleason for a glass of Moxie.

A patient in the soap opera, "General Hospital," is told: "You're okay; you've got moxie." On the recently introduced "That's My Line," Bob Barker's guest—who teaches chutzpah—asked the audience what they thought "chutzpah" meant. Immediately, a man in the back of the hall hollered "Moxie!"

It is conceivable that, someday, Moxie might no longer be available to sustain the faithful Moxie Drinkers—even in New

England. "Perish forbid!" they exclaim. Still, the flavor has been tampered with, by brewers as well as by that government bureau. Some first sippers of modern Moxie have paraphrased Peggy Lee and sighed: "Is that all there is to Moxie?" Be that as it may, the word is with us and it is very unlikely that it will ever die. In the sweet bye and bye, some post-nuclear-age archeologist digging through the atomic rubble may unearth one of those old embossed Moxie bottles and exclaim: "How clever of them to have named a product 'Moxie!'"

But just how did "moxie" come to mean what it does? Very simply, the basic meaning (nervy) of the word was born when Dr. Augustin Thompson's Moxie Nerve Food began to push its way past the palates of the populace. Thereafter, whenever anyone exhibited an uncommon amount of nerve, he was said to be "full of Moxie."

CHAPTER 5

Of Bottles
and Battles

A product's container sometimes contains other than the product. In the early days of television, it was not uncommon to see commercials in which oversized consumer-goods boxes, with legs protruding, danced in front of the cameras. Large replicas of the product itself have walked the streets with a person inside—as in the case of the popular Planters Peanut Man. Huge cans mounted on automobile chassis, such as the Vanish Van and the V-8 Cocktail Roadster, are eye-catchers; but no mobilized units were more startling than the contraptions that rolled the roads for Moxie.

One of the earliest mobile advertisements was the turn-of-the-century Moxie Bottle Wagon. This four-wheeled wonder was pulled by a single horse and, perched high up front above the fifth wheel, was a Moxie Man driver. Slung low between large-diameter rear wheels stood an eight-foot-tall replica of the Moxie bottle looking for all the world like the upright boiler of a steam fire engine. Lettering on this gigantic bottle read: MOXIE NERVE FOOD...DELICIOUS AND HEALTHFUL...FEEDS THE NERVES. On the bottle's high shoulder appeared the words: FUN TO DRINK—a daring claim in sober-sided New England. Through a door in the back of the bottle, a Moxie Man could dispense Moxie: ICE COLD 5¢ per GLASS.

In the August, 1969, issue of *Yankee* magazine, Edna Hills Humphrey's "The Moxie Man" tells how her father, Charles E. Hills, a vacationing Dartmouth medical student, spent the spring of 1899 driving a Moxie Bottle Wagon.

"This was the era of huge profits from the sale of patent medicines such as Hood's Sarsaparilla and Father John's Medicine," wrote Mrs. Humphrey. Huge profits for Mr. Hood, Father John and Doctor Thompson perhaps; and we can believe it when we know a little about how much of the gross take went for certain expenses—at least in the case of Charlie Hills, the Moxie Man, who sallied forth in the raw New England weather for dear Doctor Thompson. . . upon rugged roads. . . in an open wagon. . . to spend his nights in such hotels as he could find.

"Father's careful record shows," Mrs. Humphrey goes on, "that he spent the first night at the Hotel Fitchburg at a cost of $2.50. This included the stabling and feeding of his horse as well as his own supper and breakfast. . . The Hotel Springfield charged $5.50. In some towns it was only $1.50. . . He often wrote 'good' or 'bum' in his notebook after the name of a hotel. . . His expenses for the first week (paid by the company) came to $19.05. In addition, his salary was a full $12.00!. . . The item 'nails' appears several times. These were for tacking Moxie signs on trees. Once, Father was about to tack a sign to a tree in Wellesley Farms, just across the bridge over the Charles River, when a constable rushed up and told him that such advertising was not permitted in Wellesley. My father knew that the other end of the bridge was in Newton, and took great delight in going across the bridge and tacking the sign up there."

Also, in his notebook, Charlie commented "very hard roads," meaning poor, regarding his route. But, you ask, didn't he have all that free Moxie to give him the old zip? It's a lot to swallow, but honest Charlie Hills often entered Moxie at five, ten and even fifteen cents as a personal expense in his record.

Later on, the fabulous Moxie horsemobiles (Moxiemobiles) appeared. These vehicles were automobile chassis mounting dummy horses and were driven from the saddle. Their construction did not include a large bottle; nevertheless they often accompanied sound tracks carrying Moxie bottles approximately six to eight feet high. Sometimes a large Moxie bottle could be seen riding erect in the bed of a pickup truck.

The largest Moxie bottle ever built still exists. On its concrete foundation it reared its white, metal cap some sixty feet toward the sky in Pine Island Amusement Park near Manchester, New Hampshire. It was erected next to the bridge that led to the mainland and was part of a free-sample beverage stand The Moxie Company had there at the turn of the century. When this edifice was finally abandoned the bottle was taken apart, hauled across the

It was possible for Charlie Hills to hide inside the bottle when it rained. Photo courtesy of Yankee *magazine and Edna Hills Humphrey.*

pond one winter on the ice and assembled on a spot about a mile from its original location. Now only thirty-five feet tall (without its elevating foundation) it became part of a one-story camp that was eventually bought by James A. Todd.

"We were looking for a place with good spring water for our baby in 1922," said Mrs. Todd, "and that's how we arrived in Manchester. At that time the bottle had already been built into the

"My mother would always let me slide down inside the big bottle in the Pine Island Park and have a drink of Moxie."—Mrs. Dorothy Wilson of Houston, Texas.

camp and we bought the place. The bottle's made of teak wood and all bolted together. We had it finished off inside and it's in very good shape." There are three bedrooms in this three-storied

The label has been shingled over, but most folks know it as The Old Moxie Bottle House.

bottle, the upper ones reached by ladders. Each room has its own window.

"Motorists are constantly stopping by the house," Mrs. Todd said. "They always ask the same questions. First off, they want to know what we've got inside the bottle. Then they want us to tell them how we ended up owning a Moxie house."

James Todd, now a retired newspaper executive, said that they use the place as a summer home and live in Silver Spring, Maryland, during the rest of the year. "Life in a Moxie bottle isn't quite as uncomfortable as it may seem," he said. "My wife Mary and I love the place. Our children—we had four of them—loved it. It's quite a thing for a youngster to live in a Moxie bottle."

Mr. Todd added that he has received "dozens of offers for the house," but turned them all down. "After all," he smiled, "how many people own a Moxie bottle house? Besides, it's easy to give directions to the place. All you hve to do is tell friends to look for the Moxie bottle."

If Shakespeare had known about Moxie, he probably wouldn't have asked "What's in a name?" Such was the popularity of Moxie that many other firms decided to cash in on Moxie's

THIS
BOOK
ABOUT
SUBSTITUTION
LAW.

Published by

THE *Moxie* COMPANY OF AMERICA

EXECUTIVE OFFICES

260 TREMONT STREET : : BOSTON, MASS.

A LITTLE HISTORY
OF MANY BIG CASES

We present in this book a short history of some important cases, which we hope you will read and consider carefully.

The Moxie Company is vigilant in protecting its trade rights and in giving to every MOXIE user, protection against unfair competition and substitution, at any cost.

Several of these cases were fought to the highest Courts, and the results are clear-cut decisions, which are of interest:

To every established and reputable maker of a well-known product;

To every dealer selling such a product; and

To every consumer who knows what he orders and pays for.

Great credit is due to our attorneys in these cases, OLIVER MITCHELL, ESQ., of Boston, and his associate, JOSEPH T. BRENNAN, ESQ., for the skilful and conscientious manner in which all our litigation in trade mark and patent cases has been conducted. The problems presented to them were not easy to solve and the satisfactory results are well attested by a reading of the decisions in this book.

THE MOXIE COMPANY

success. Several of them endeavored to adopt names too similar to Moxie to sit well with Dr. Thompson and his ambitious associates. Equally annoying to the Moxie people was the substitution of other products when Moxie was called for by customers. The situation is well put forth in a 64-page pamphlet published by The Moxie Company of America titled "This Book About Substitution Law," which contained "A Little History of Many Big Cases."

Preface

This book has been prepared primarily for the purpose of answering oft-repeated inquiries for information as to the Moxie trade-mark, bottles, glasses, packages, signs, symbols, slogans, inventions, designs and other insignia identified with the Moxie business.

During the last forty odd years, The Moxie Company and its predecessors have expended much effort and money in introducing Moxie to the public and in establishing its legal rights in its trademark and the trade name Moxie, with the result that millions of people know and like Moxie, and it is in demand everywhere.

This is what we have worked for and this confidence and public demand for Moxie has become an asset of tremendous value: the Goodwill of our business.

There is another result, however, of the great demand for Moxie, which seems inseparable from popularity as shadow is inseparable from sunshine, namely: that unscrupulous manufacturers and dealers sometimes substitute spurious imitations when Moxie is called for, imitate Moxie as closely as they are able in color and taste, and imitate the bottle of Moxie, considered as a package, with its label, shape, color and distinctive appearance.

The Moxie Company has waged war on this form of trade piracy for years,—not because it lives to fight, as some of its opponents have declared—but because it has found it necessary to fight to live, and to protect the public from the substitutors.

An exceedingly efficient organization has been developed for discovering substitutors and suppressing them promptly when discovered. Numerous injunctions covering many different forms of unfair trade have been granted by Federal and State courts on our complaints against infringers. These adjudications we have summarized and collected in this book,

THE
DISTINCTIVE
MOXIE
BOTTLE

UNIQUE IN
DESIGN AND
APPEARANCE

REGISTERED
AND PROTECTED
BY FEDERAL AND
STATE COURTS
IN NUMEROUS
DECISIONS

MOXIE
SHIPPING CASE

Wib Its Slip-on
Bottle Protector
Designed
and Patented by

Frank M. Archer, for use on Moxie bottles only

83

believing that such a collection is the best means of informing Dealers, Salespeople and the public of what is not permissible in trade competition.

INJUNCTIONS have been issued against many classes of persons handling imitations of Moxie, including Beverage Manufacturers, Manufacturing Chemists, Bottlers, Apothecaries, Proprietors of Hotels, Restaurants, Refreshment Booths, Grocery Stores, Fruit and Confectionery Stores, former Moxie Agents, and Dispensers in stores where infringements of Moxie were sold.

The acts forbidden under the injunctions included Substitution of other beverages when Moxie was called for; Sale of spurious beverages with the Suggestion to dealers that they can be used for the purpose of Substitution as and for Moxie; Refilling of Moxie bottles with a spurious beverage; Use of various names or trade marks infringing upon The Moxie Company's trade name and trademark Moxie; Use of labels in imitation of the Moxie labels; Making and sale of a beverage similar to Moxie in taste, color, etc. in a package similar to the Moxie package; Sale of a beverage in a bottle which, in size, proportions, color and shape, resembles the bottle of Moxie; use of a bottle like the Moxie bottle; Use of imitative Crown Seals; Use of Moxie glasses for other beverages; Display of Moxie advertising matter where no Moxie is, in fact, for sale; and the making of a syrup to be used in preparing a substitute for Moxie. In many cases the infringing beverages, syrups and bottles were ordered to be delivered up for destruction.

Among names imitative of Moxie the following are found: PROXIE, HOXIE, NOXIE, NOXIE NERVE TONIC, NOXALL, NERV-E-ZA, NON-TOX, APPETIZER, VISNER, PURO, NICKLE-TONE, NEURENE, NERVE FOOD (Standard, East India, Excelsior, Imperial), MILLER, MAN-OLA, MODOX, RIXIE, TOXIE, etc. etc.

A few of the distinctive marks and insignia of The Moxie Company will be found reproduced herein and some of the infringements referred to in the Decrees of the Courts.

In addition to the Moxie Company's exceedingly efficient organization for discovering imitators, the company also had the help of loyal Moxie Drinkers. Moxie's Substitution Law pamphlet contained the following quaint correspondence:

A Typical Instance of a Customer's Vigilance
and the Result

Cathance Lake, Cooper, Maine
August 13, 1917

The Moxie Company,
Dear Sirs:
On August seventh I bought three bottles of Moxie at Harry Lombard's store, in Meddybemps, Maine. When I got them back to the camp I noticed they were *without* labels and each bottle had the same sort of cap to it. (I am sending you one of the caps.) One of the bottles was without doubt a regulation Moxie bottle, stamped with your mark, but the other two were marked "Four Crown Soda Water, Clark's Harbor, N.S., M.A. Nickerson." They all contained the same kind of drink (imitation Moxie) which made two members of the party extremely ill for about six hours.

We have been drinking Moxie all our lives and it has never before made us ill.

I do not wish to make any claims but I do hope that you will follow this up, for the vile stuff was bottled in one of your bottles which I will be glad to send you upon your request. My reason for writing this is to save someone else from a similar experience.

Very sincerely yours,
S. F. SHAW.

The Moxie Company immediately dispatched an inspector to interview Mr. Lombard in Meddybemps and learned that he was selling a beverage put up by Walter J. Commins, of Calais, Maine, which had the appearance of Moxie. "Of course," The Moxie Company's letter to Miss Sarah F. Shaw related," as is usual in such cases, he (Mr. Lombard) denied having sold any of the Commins beverage upon a call for Moxie."

The Moxie Company then sent their Mr. Brennan to Calais on August 25th, where he conferred with Mr. Commins and his attorney, Richard J. Garrigle, Esquire. The result of Mr. Brennan's visit was that The Moxie Company put a quick and effective stop to the infringement on their rights. Commins admitted that he had, indeed, made and sold the infringing beverage, and signed a written agreement to immediately stop "the putting up and sale of such beverage," coupled with a provision for the destruction of the imitation Moxie bottles. Moxie also exacted a similar agreement from Mr. Lombard and told him that a letter of apology was due Sarah Shaw together with an agreement to pay her and her party for "any medical service or otherwise on account of the sale of this spurious beverage" to her.

Note that it took only twelve days from Miss Shaw's posting of her letter until this incident was settled. Other infringement cases were also dealt with speedily and summarily. The wallop of Moxie, it seems, was not confined to the drink itself.

Today, little is known about these imitation Moxies; and since only a limited amount of such spurious products was produced, and because most of the imitation Moxie bottles were destroyed, those few bottles which survived are rare and valuable indeed— and are being quietly sought by knowledgeable Moxiana collectors and dealers.

Both Toxie and Proxie attempted to copyright their names, but Moxie prevailed against them.

Modox was perhaps Moxie's closest rival (as "The Great Nerve and Health Beverage...Made from Indian Tonic Herbs"). Modox signs and trays are still being found. Visner's Nox-All bottles were ordered destroyed "whether full or empty."

Besides being nearby imitators of Moxie, these Lynn and Salem tonics competed against each other as "Invigorating, Refreshing, Healthful" appetizers. Both had pictures of witches on their labels.

Two imitators of Moxie, declared by the courts to be infringements and restrained by injunction proceedings.

Two counterfeits found in Canada. Several firms in the United States, as well, were enjoined from selling any beverage under the name of "Moxie" not manufactured by The Moxie Company.

CHAPTER 6

"Oh Glorious Ride!"

The very first automobile ever seen in many towns may have had "Moxie" lettered on its sides. By the end of the first decade of the twentieth century the Moxie autos had become a familiar sight on the roads of seventeen states and the Moxie Man was considered to be a highly experienced automobilist. The public relations value of its drivers did not go unexploited by The Moxie Company.

In their gauntlets and goggles, these intrepid travelers had become the heroes of the small fry and the confidants of their dads. Just to be seen talking with a Moxie Man was a feather in the caps of fathers and sons alike. To know something about "machines" meant status; and all the cries of "Get a horse!" did not diminish the pride of knowing which pedals to push in a horseless carriage. "Devils Wagons," they were often called; and devil-may-care was the spirit of the day. Arguments frequently arose over which type of automobile was the best: gasoline, electric or steam; and Moxie had them all.

In 1910, Victor Appleton's exceedingly popular *Tom Swift and His Electric Runabout . . . Or the Speediest Car on the Road* was published. At the same time, Jas. A. Braden's "Auto Boys" adventures were being read in school—hidden behind those big geography books. Just about anything anybody wrote about automobiles was loftily quoted by any chap who called himself a red-blooded American; and red-blooded was the Moxie Man image. No run-of-the-mill drummer, he. He was healthy, certainly, and courteous, dependable, self-respecting, cooperative and daring. In 1908, the Boy Scouts of America had been founded; and the Moxie Man was a scout's oath type of man, a leader.

There could not have been a more auspicious time for The Moxie Company to publish the following pamphlet than at the beginning of the second decade of this fabulous century of burgeoning mobility, January 1, 1911.

We and our representatives on the road are often requested to give information and in fact, in many instances, to give demonstrations of the practicability of automobiles from both a business and a private standpoint.

As we are undoubtedly the pioneers in the use of automobiles in a large way, for selling, advertising and delivery, it is not to be wondered at that we and our men have acquired some information along these lines during the long period we have been using automobiles; information which may be as helpful as it is interesting, as interesting as it is unusual, in some of its details.

It is therefore possible that some of the statistics relative to the operation of Moxie autos will be appreciated by our millions of friends.

The automobile has long ago reached that stage of perfection which makes it practical in every respect, and a person may safely buy any of the well-known cars from any reliable manufacturer who is known to stand by his product, and feel assured that it will prove successful, provided, of course, he will give it the attention it deserves.

The principal thing is to see that the car is properly cleaned, oiled and greased, that it has a sufficient supply of gasoline and that it is driven and handled in a reasonable manner. Do not try to re-design the car. The designer and manufacturer have attended to that. Follow their instructions in its operation and maintenance and your difficulties will be slight.

We believe that by doing our business with automobiles we are able to engage a much better class of men.

The health of the men is better than if they were obliged to travel in any other manner, due not only to the fact that they are enabled to be in the open air so much but because they are able to select and reach better sleeping and eating accommodations, than they could were they dependent upon the usual means of conveyance.

Moxie autos have enabled the Moxie men to visit, put up and distribute Moxie advertising matter, etc., in thousands of places where it would have been impracticable and almost impossible to have gone in any other way.

By means of automobiles we have been able to do from four to six times as much work in a day, as by any other means and therefore to do it at from one-quarter to one-sixth the cost of any other method.

None of our men have ever been injured in an accident in operating Moxie autos.

The advent of the Moxie auto in a community is an introduction to the customer which it would be difficult to secure by any other means.

The vast experience of the men who travel by the Moxie autos renders them automobile experts as it were, inasmuch as each customer wants to know all about the car, how much it costs, how much gasoline it uses, what tires are the best, what car is the best and in fact, asks every conceivable question relative to automobiles, their uses, expense of up-keep, etc. Very frequently the men are asked to demonstrate their car, not only for the Moxie customers but for their families, and for the public in general, which is always interested.

The Moxie men, however, are always in good

health and spirits and pride themselves on their courtesy. It is always a pleasure for them to compare notes with anyone or give any information they may have relative to autos, hotels, garages, or places. As to roads, also, they become authorities, and wherever they reach a hotel at night as well as the garage where they put up, there are always many tourists who are anxious to obtain reliable data on these points, and the Moxie Man is always referred to.

But a short time ago a school teacher in a small town, in one of the many States covered by the Moxie autos requested the "Moxie Man" to visit the school and give a demonstration or a lecture, as it were, to her class, on the operation of an automobile.

Why we speak of "The Moxie Man" in referring to one of our salesmen is that their own names are scarcely ever remembered by their customers and others who interview them and they are in consequence most commonly addressed, "The Moxie Man."

The Moxie automobiles are familiar to everyone in all of the parades that are continuously being given in the thousands of towns and cities visited by them; in fact, no parade is a success without the Moxie car as a show-feature.

The Moxie car blazed the way through thousands of miles of country roads which were probably never before traveled by automobiles.

The Moxie Company, years ago, at great expense, assisted the automobilist by putting up signs in different localities, giving the name of the nearest town and the distance thereto.

Undoubtedly, by operating automobiles, the Moxie Company has done much to encourage and demonstrate to the public the advantages of Good Roads.

Garages throughout the country regard it as an honor to have an opportunity to take care of the Moxie auto when it is in town. It increases the prestige of the garage with the townspeople, for, as has often been remarked, "If it's good enough for the Moxie car, it's good enough for any car."

The Moxie Company has never had a serious accident with any of its many autos.

One of the Moxie salesmen, writing in, said, "Traveling as I do with the Moxie Auto often brings to my mind thoughts of my friends and acquaintances whose occupation is the selling and advertising of various wares, but who are less fortunate than I, as they travel in smoky, stuffy, steam cars. They complain of lack of appetite, loss of vitality, effected nerves and many other ills. They are always sighing for fresh air. Thank Heaven, I am not leading such a life. I have gained twenty pounds in weight since I commenced operating the Moxie car. I am in perfect condition in every respect and capable of doing two men's work with pleasure."

The Moxie men all take pride in their cars and give them the attention they deserve. For that reason they are always in operation.

Some of the Moxie autos are going every day of the year, in all kinds of localities and over roads of all conditions. They have, however, never found a road so difficult that they were unable to get through on time. In recent years, very little delay has been caused through repairs, etc.

When the Moxie salesman arrives at a store, he has a full line of advertising matter, etc., with him and can therefore, give the dealer most prompt attention and put up the advertising matter then and there.

When the Moxie man has finished his work

in a town he does not have to wait for the stage-coach, steam cars, trolley or any other mode of travel, but may be on his way without delay.

The Moxie autos are equipped to enable the men to travel under the very best conditions and with the maximum of comfort in all seasons. There is, therefore, no weather so bad but that the Moxie man can reach his customer and is not obliged to remain in the hotel or other places waiting for "favorable" conditions.

The Moxie car has become a feature at all the great as well as the small Fairs throughout the country, and is regularly solicited to give "exhibition-miles."

The Moxie auto and the Moxie men are treated very generously by all the theatrical people, moving-picture shows, etc., as well as by the newspapers, but to refer to the thousands upon thousands of these clippings, notices, pictures, etc., would not be justified by the space at hand. As an illustration, however, we print from The Norway (Oxford County, Me.) Advertiser of September 23, 1910:

A MILE A MINUTE
Advertiser Man Made Record Auto Trip in the "Moxie"
on the Oxford County Fair Track.

To ride in the famous "Moxie" automobile around the track at the annual county fair was the good fortune of the ADVERTISER reporter. The mile was made in the remarkable time of 1.44, and the greater part of the mighty speed contest was at better than a mile a minute clip. Invited as the special guest of Lewis St. John in the 30 horsepower "Buick" automobile the reporter had the rare pleasure of making this fast time, Wednesday.

If you are looking for a sport that will send the red blood coursing through your veins at a gallop and set every nerve a-tingle, let me advise you confidently that you can find all this in less than a minute and a half by the side of Mr. St. John, on the Oxford County Fair grounds. It's a start, a rapid whiz through the air, a confusion of faces, as the thousands that line the track are passed, then the cheering of the crowds on the grandstand and a grinding of brakes. Like some mighty monster brought to bay the powerful automobile stops, gracefully, under the skillful guidance of Mr. St. John.

For the man who has never traveled a mile a minute in a racing automobile, the brief space of a minute and forty-four seconds with Mr. St. John was indeed a revelation.

When one comes to consider that the "Moxie" automobile is heavily loaded and that the curves of the Oxford County track are very sharp for such speed, the time made was really marvelous. Sitting in the luxurious automobile at ease among the cushions, one feels practically no sensation except the whiz through space. There is no jar from the motor or engine—the old time rumble of early model machines, is an unknown quantity in this 20th century marvel.

Around the curves the power is shut off; then when the straight track is reached it's a mighty whiz through the air for a few seconds at fully a 75 mile-a-minute clip, watching the road ahead, on—on—at a rapid speed.

A glorious ride! There is no motion or jar—it is like the graceful glide of a sled upon a smooth snow clad hillside.

HARRY A. PACKARD

We have been using automobiles for about ten years.

Number of automobiles used, fifty-four (54) including steam, electric and gasoline, of Foreign and American manufacture.

The operation of our autos has been confined to about seventeen (17) States.

The number of Cities, Towns, Villages and Four-Corners visited by the Moxie autos is more than 40,000.

It is estimated that the Moxie cars have called upon, solicited trade from, and put up advertising matter, etc., on more than a quarter of a million stores.

The number of people thus made familiar with the Moxie auto is more than 40,000,000.

The amount of Gasoline consumed by Moxie autos would practically equal a railroad train-load of 45 cars, each car loaded on the basis of the minimum carload capacity of 30,000 pounds, or approximately 158,642 gallons (660 tons).

The Rubber tires and Inner-tubes used by the Moxie autos represent a weight of more than 25 tons, or about 5½ carloads, (approximately 2700 tires).

For greasing the Moxie autos it has required about 1000 pails of grease and they have used about 4935 gallons of oil or more than 41,000 lbs. (more than 20 tons).

The cost of Moxie autos, their operation and up-keep, would amount in dollars and cents to a sum more than equal to the cost of erecting a substantial modern fireproof "sky-scraper" office-building.

The greatest distance made by a Moxie auto in the usual course of a day's business, was 211 miles. That car visited many towns, enabled our representative to all on a multitude of customers and to put out much advertising matter, etc.

The total mileage of the Moxie cars has equalled a distance of more than fifty-one (51) times around the earth.

It is estimated that to have traveled an equal distance over such character of territory as covered by the Moxie autos, and accomplished the same results in any other manner (such as by railroad, trolley, steam-boat, stage, pack-mule, etc.,) would have necessitated an outlay of money sufficient to erect several modern sky-scraper office buildings.

Issued January 1, 1911 by The Moxie Company

In Volume No. 2 we may give our experiences with different cars, to what extent the manufacturers looked after them; also dealing with the various makes of tires, inner-tubes, tools and accessories used by us, and with the treatment we have received in repair shops and garages.

Mrs. Dorothy Robinson Wilson of Houston, Texas, remembers the early Moxie autos:

"My dad, Wilder M. Robinson, was employed by The Moxie Company when they were located in Boston, Massachusetts, across the street from the North Station. I think he was associated with them from about 1904 or 1905, when I was three or four years old.

"He was still with them when I was in high school in Manchester, New Hampshire, and was asked to write a paper about the manufacture of Moxie.

"My father took me to the Moxie factory in Boston where I met an executive by the name of Thompson; I cannot be sure of his first name. I also met the next man in authority—whom I shall never forget—Frank Archer.

"Mr. Archer took me all over the plant, including the top floor—which was where the secret process was. I wrote a very good paper about the manufacture of Moxie, which was printed in the school paper.

"My father was given several Moxie autos, but he couldn't operate them, so he was furnished drivers. One of them was Carl Hager; others were Wilber Frankelton and Lester Moore.

"When I was about five years old, my father took me on one of his sales trips which covered the middle west. I remember Ohio best. One of his wholesalers, in Dayton, was Charles Terry—and I still correspond with Mr. Terry's daughter, who is in her middle eighties.

"Just one thing more. At one time I had a large picture of Moxie autos leaving on a tour from Boston to New York—and they were electrics."

Little Miss Dorothy and her dog, Aga, in Daddy's Moxie auto, a 1905 Rambler. Notice the early treatment of the Moxie logotype. The box on the back, with its "captain's walk" railing around the top, was used on many later Moxie autos. As with many early automobiles, this one had tread only on the rear tires.

Most early American automobiles were right-hand drive. This is a 1908 Buick. Moustachioed Mr. Robinson is seated to the left; his driver, Carl Hagar, is behind the wheel. Notice the Moxie "feather tickle" cutout sign on the running board.

These Buick pickup trucks had windshields—perhaps suggested by Wilder Robinson. The poster lad on the running boards of the autos to the right is the same one as in the "feather tickle" sign.

CHAPTER 7

Building a Better Moxiemobile

The eye-catching appeal and intrigue of a mobile dummy horse was exploited long before the Moxiemobiles made their appearance. Virgil's *Aeneid* tells us how the colossal hollow figure of a horse was rolled into Troy as a gift. At night, warriors sneaked out of this wooden horse and opened the gates of the city to admit the Greek army.

As the twentieth century approached—and the transition from horse-drawn to self-propelled vehicles got underway—some curious inventions attempted to ease the shock of the passage. Even the idea of mechanizing the horse itself was not beyond imagination. On February 29, 1888, the weekly *Five Cent Wide Awake Library* published "The Electric Horse" written by someone who, for whatever clandestine reason, signed this magnum opus "Noname."

In 1899, while Charlie Hills was driving his Moxie Bottle Wagon through New England, the Haynes-Apperson Company of Kokomo, Indiana, produced a vehicle of startling appearance—although the idea was to make a motorcar that wouldn't startle horses. The invention was the brain child of Uriah Smith of Battle Creek, Michigan. A stuffed horse's head and chest was to be mounted on the front of a previously "horseless" carriage. This was supposed to create the illusion of a horse and buggy, and thus fool approaching live horses so that they would not panic and rear up, possibly even break and run, as they so often did when confronted by these strange new, noisy contraptions.

Elmer Apperson thought the ruse might work, so he had a bust of old Dobbin fastened to the front of a new Haynes-Apperson motor surry. John Landon (husband of Mary Landon, a

101

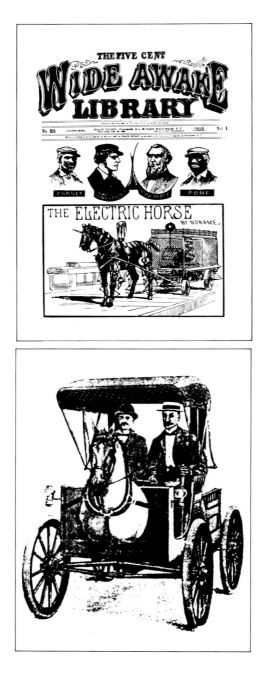

Apperson's Folly. Information and photograph through courtesy of automobile historian Stanley Yost and the Wayside Press.

company office worker) was volunteered to take this novel vehicle for a drive in the country to find out whether or not the interloper would be accepted as one of their own by the Indiana horses; it wasn't!

The experiment was judged "not satisfactory." Uriah returned, with nagging doubts, to Battle Creek. The horse's bust remained for many months at the Haynes-Apperson works—giving rise to much ribaldry, but never in the presence of Mr. Apperson, who finally consigned the hapless horse's head to whatever pastures such follies go.

Perhaps the tremendous appeal of a horsemobile will never disappear. Even today, happy toddlers still straddle Kiddie Kars and propel themselves along behind the painted figure heads of horses; and horses are still the favorite mounts on that mechanical marvel, the merry-go-round.

And so it was for fun that Miles Harold Carpenter, in his late 20s, agreed to build a horsemobile for The Moxie Company. Neither "Hal" nor The Moxie Company had any desire to fool anyone. It was mainly for amusement and, naturally, to keep the name of Moxie in the minds of the multitude.

The idea of mounting a full dummy horse on an automobile chassis did not originate with Hal Carpenter. It had been a hot flash in Frank Archer's effervescent brain. Apparently Mr. Archer, et al, had already constructed a horsemobile on a light automobile chassis, and then Archer had it patented on February 27, 1917. A photograph of this Moxiemobile, appearing on page 67 of a brochure for the 1917 Boston Automobile Show, is identical to the one depicted in the patent drawing. Just when this first (if, indeed, it was the first) Moxiemobile was built has not been discovered; it must have been in 1915 or possibly earlier. In appearance, the chassis resembles that of a Saxon or Metz. Toy metal Moxiemobiles have been found, reportedly dated 1916, which were definitely patterned after this full-sized horsemobile. Clumsy and top-heavy though it may have been, this advertising vehicle was a tremendous success, and The Moxie Company was very anxious to have another like it—but better.

"For several years," says Hal, "the Moxie people in Boston had been trying to motorize one of their sales gimmicks, a black horse carrying a red-coated hunter who rode from town to town promoting their tonic. They'd found that mounting a dummy horse on an automobile chassis was possible, but that it was unsafe, if not foolhardy, for anyone to attempt to drive such a rig while sitting atop the horse. Well, one day Fred Wright, who was then the Auburn and Dort dealer in New York, asked me to tackle the job—just for kicks.

Fig. 1.

The driver is wearing a Moxiecloth jacket. Similar garments still survive. Bolts of one design of this cloth have been found.

This photograph was taken in Canandaigua, New York. Clarence Horner of Toledo, Ohio, says that it was given to him over fifty years ago by an aunt in Newark, Ohio. It appeared on the inside back cover of the March-April, 1970, issue of Antique Automobile.

"What with automobiles putting an end to the heyday of the horse, it was easy to find a hard-up harness maker willing to sell me the dummy horse he used for displaying his wares. I cut off the horse's legs a bit, beefed up the body with some internal reinforcements and mounted the beast on a Dort Speedster chassis.

(The dummy horse used for the Carpenter Moxiemobile was constructed of papiermache; several of this type were used for the earlier rigs. At least one was different, however. Mrs. Paul Ballotte of Holden, Massachusetts, says: "My Uncle Arthur owned the Tetrault Harness Shop in Worcester. When he was going out of business, The Moxie Company purchased his large wooden horse for about $75. We still have a snapshot of this horse taken while it was in the shop window. Uncle was told that the horse would be mounted on a truck to advertise Moxie and they promised to show it to him before they left for the South. The promise was kept and my aunt said it looked beautiful.")

"The steering shaft," Hal continued, "went down through the horse's neck and chest and reached the steering gear through a series of short rods and universal joints. Transmission gear shifting was accomplished from the saddle by means of an offset and extended lever. Platform stirrups were located directly behind rearranged clutch and brake pedals.

"The accelerator was my pride and joy. You placed your foot on the right-hand stirrup platform and slid it forward to move a curved-bar pedal which opened the throttle. That way, you could stand up on the stirrups and ride over rough roads without danger of being thrown off.

"When I finished putting that Moxiemobile together in a loft on 57th Street, I rode it down Broadway and wound up on Wall Street one noon hour. It stirred up as much fuss as those big-bosomed girls did there not so long ago. A giant of a traffic cop came over and told me I was in the wrong stock market for playing cowboy. He walked in front of me and opened up a lane through the crowd so that I could get my steed on its way back uptown.

"Another day, after I'd gotten so that I could handle the mount well enough, I pulled out onto Broadway again. Remember, this was 1917 and they still had trolley cars. Well, I swung onto the trolley tracks—which guided the Dort's narrow tires and kept me going straight—then I rode from 57th to 54th Street standing on my head in the saddle.

Uncle Arthur's white wooden horse was the right color for a Moxiemobile.

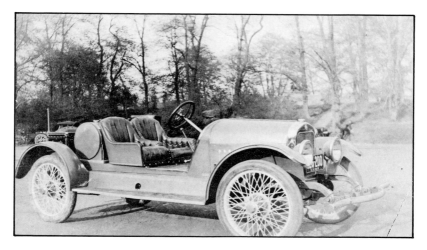

This Dort Speedster, bearing a 1917 license plate, is similar to the one used for Hal Carpenter's Moxiemobile.

"The next day, I took a tenderfoot Moxie Man out to the wild and wooly Bronx and taught him how to control the critter. It sure would give the New York kids a thrill if one of those old Moxiemobiles came down the street today. I'll bet a million people would see it on television now, instead of on the newsreels in the movie houses like they did back then."

Although the Dort Moxiemobile was at one time used to promote Greyhound Tires, it remained a safe advertising vehicle

Hal demonstrates how he drove the Dort Moxiemobile down Broadway.

The Dort Moxiemobile with its builder, Miles Harold "Hal" Carpenter. The horse was probably painted white later on.

Left-hand view showing extended clutch pedal. Note the steering-shaft universal joint protruding from the horse's chest.

Right-hand view showing the relocated brake pedal, gear-shift lever and the curved-bar accelerator beside the platform stirrup. For emergency braking, the foot-brake pedal was tilted forward to engage a ratchet.

for Moxie for quite some time. Later Moxiemobiles were constructed using white, aluminum horses made in specially built molds. The Carpenter Moxiemobile was probably the only one ever to have a black horse.

In 1932, The Moxie Company was operating Moxiemobiles using chassis from a four-cylinder and a six-cylinder Buick, three LaSalles and one Rolls-Royce. Over the years, there were other makes as well. One in particular, a sturdy if homely Essex, gave yeoman service and traveled far and wide with Mark Barker, The Daredevil of the Moxie Boys, in the saddle. Of the many Moxiemobiles once frequently seen on America's highways and in its towns and cities, only one was saved. This LaSalle—both a classic automobile and an advertising classic—was recently painstakingly restored at a cost of some $25,000 and, although not roaming the roads quite as freely as it once did, is being exhibited in parades, at county fairs and other public events, mainly in New England. There are no more lollipops, but Moxie wooden nickels are handed out. Because of inflation, perhaps, these nickels are "Good for 10¢ on a Moxie."

The last Moxiemobile, an unrestored LaSalle in use in 1957 in Dover, New Hampshire. The man at the rear of the rig is Ernest "Red" Cutter, later plant manager of Coheco Bottling Company, Rochester, New Hampshire a division of Eastern, Inc. The thirteen kids? Moxie drinkers, all!

CHAPTER 8

Yankee Doodle Moxie

The most common cry that arose whenever a Moxiemobile appeared was, "Get a horse!"—hardly an apt epithet to hurl at a horsemobile. The next most often heard remark was, "You'd never catch me on any such contraption." But what sort of an individual would really hanker to drive a Moxie horsemobile? The Moxie people certainly weren't looking for someone who'd have to be coaxed to take the job. He had to be a natural for the Yankee Doodle riding on a pony type of picture Moxie meant to present.

The ideal "Moxie Boy" would be some young adventurer whom you couldn't keep out of the saddle—a half cowboy and half clown, a consummate extrovert with a finely tuned flair for animated fantasy. The Moxie Company somehow managed to attract quite a few top-banana candidates. One of them was even known as "Moxie Bananas" Zaffiro. He is one of the half-dozen performing Moxiemobile drivers still alive at this writing. The liveliest of all, however, is Mark E. Barker—now living it up in Arizona. Although he claims to be "semi-retired," he was discovered, in 1979, running the Mesa Junior Miss Pageant.

"Pretty girls?" he laughed, "Why not? I'm only 76. Now you don't have to call me Mister Barker, and you don't have to call me Mark; but you can call me Moxo if you like, because that's who I've been for years, Moxo, the Magician. That's how it reads on my car's license plate: MOXO. About my having been a Moxie Boy? Tell you what I'm gonna do. I'm gonna start with what happened to me at the ripe old age of nineteen, on October twentieth in nineteen hundred and twenty-two, to be exact.

"I was with Harry Orr's Society Circus—really a horse show—at the Commonwealth Armory in Boston. I'd ridden a lot

111

*"Moxo" Barker in his Moxiecloth clown suit on St. Patrick's Day. The little
fellow with him? Probably a leprechaun.*

already; had my own cow pony down in Presque Isle, Maine, where I was born. Now, I was with the 110th Cavalry and doing a western act, spinning a hundred-foot rope around a horse while standing in the saddle. I was also the producing clown, which meant that I was in charge of all the other clowns and produced the acts we did.

"Well, after the show a man by the name of Frank Morton Archer came backstage and asked me if I'd like to join The Moxie Company and go around to winter carnivals and such as his Moxie Clown. The way it turned out, I also did a lot of entertaining at children's hospitals, especially for Mr. Archer.

"He was really something! Remember those Moxie Man signs—the ones with that man pointing right at you and saying 'Drink Moxie!'? I suppose you've heard that this Moxie Man was none other than Frank Archer himself. It was probably the most famous commercial sign ever made. It made folks drink Moxie because Frank Archer told them to. The expression 'Frank Archer says!' had clout. He was like E. F. Hutton; whenever Frank Archer spoke, everybody paid attention.

"To get back to doing my act at those children's hospitals. Mr. Archer was always interested in kids, especially the ones who'd got laid up somehow or were poor or orphans. Every year, he got out his Moxie autos and trucks and fetched kids to Nantasket Beach and such places for outings. He liked newsboys too; gave them carloads of carts; in the winter, he gave them sleds. Mr. Archer also treated the folks who worked for him real good, but he didn't think of them as his employees. 'We have no laborers, no help, no employees,' he said, 'Everybody here is an associate.' There are still some of those Waltham watches around with 'Moxie Associate' inscribed on them.

"Mr. Archer was born in Lincoln, Maine, and came to Boston as a lad with only twenty-three dollars to his name. He went to work as an office boy in an electrical firm, then he went on to become a salesman and then bookkeeper. He was a regular Horatio Alger hero. In time, he became interested in The Moxie Company and finally gained control of it. When he died, he was Moxie's chairman of the board and a lot of other things. The theater was his hobby. He got to be personal friends with George M. Cohan, Jack Donahue, Ed Wynn, Raymond Hitchcock and several other stars. He had a couple dozen honorary pallbearers at his funeral including Cohan and Governor James M. Curley.

"When Mr. Archer hired me as a clown he must've also had my horsemanship in mind because, the next year, he asked me if I'd like to be one of his Moxie Boys and drive a Moxiemobile. I didn't have a driver's license, so he arranged for me to go out on one of his trucks and learn how to drive. That was the hardest work I ever did, carrying cases of Moxie into the cellars of stores and learning how to drive that old White truck. For a month, I rode with one of Mr. Archer's toughest old-time truckers, who kicked at me whenever I got the itch to bear down too hard on the gas. His hobnail boots kept my ankles black and blue.

"Finally, I won my spurs. With my tenderfoot's driving license in my pocket, I was taken over to the stables—I mean garage—to see my mount. There she was! A shining white horse atop a spanking new Essex chassis. Looking at snapshots I still have of that old Essex, I see that it had the lines of an army tank—and it drove like one—but I thought it was the most beautiful thing I'd ever laid eyes on. I could hardly wait to drive my splendid steed home and show it off to my mother and all my relatives.

"My first assignment was to try to get into a parade that was to take place the following week in Boston during the National Elks Convention. (Later, on June 17, 1923, we had a couple of the Moxie 'horses' at the dedication of the 'Elk on the Trail' memorial statue at Whitcomb's Summit on the Mohawk Trail.) This Elks' parade was the first time I was to try my hand at getting into an event uninvited; but it sure wasn't the last.

"Thousands of people were already lining the streets waiting for the parade to start when I began to move my mount along the route, wondering how I'd be able to muscle my way into the procession. Good-natured Irish cops waved to me but warned me that I'd better get lost before the parade started.

"Suddenly, I heard a tremendous yell rise up from about a hundred wild Texas cowpokes who were forming their lines to march in the parade—but without horses. They'd spied me and my white mustang. 'Boys!' their leader hollered, 'We've found a maverick to lead us.' When I tried to explain that the police wouldn't let me in the parade because I had an advertising vehicle, I might just as well have been whistling 'Dixie'. They slammed a big Stetson hat on my noggin; about ten of them climbed aboard the chassis under the horse; and we were off and running at the head of their division.

"A sergeant of police came roaring up on his motorbike and

AT THE DEDICATION OF THE "ELK ON THE TRAIL" MEMORIAL

When the Benevolent and Protective Order of Elks of This State Unveiled the Monument to the Elks, Who Participated in the World War, at Whitcomb's Summit, Greenfield, Mass., on Sunday, June 17th, Over 15,000 Members of That Association Were in Attendance. A Line of Automobiles for 35 Miles Extended Along the Mohawk Trail. This Picture Shows a Fractional Part of the Great Crowd Singing "America" Immediately After the Unveiling of the Monument.

June 30 1923.

Sunday rotogravure photo of Elk dedication. The Moxiemobile is Mark Barker's Essex.

ordered me out of line. I never did see what became of the cycle. The next thing I knew, those cavorting cowhands had grabbed the sergeant, plopped a ten-gallon lid on his hot head , and parked him on the hood of that sturdy Essex. Talk about pleasing the crowd! We were still in the parade, but that wasn't enough for those Texas terrors. Nothing less than being at the head of the whole shebang was going to be good enough for them. By now, I had decided that I was about to become The Daredevil of the Moxiemobile Drivers, so I pulled out of line and passed everybody until I got up to the Mayor of Boston and the official color guard. That's where I had the good sense to swing into line again—with the rest of that five-mile parade behind us.

"The Pathe News picked us up with their newsreel cameras and The Moxie Company got a boodle of publicity for free. Naturally, Mr. Archer gave me a raise. Like that famous Stutz Bearcat, I'd managed to make good in a day. Was I ever pumped up! Hey! I was gung ho enough to tackle even New York City.

"That's where Frank Archer sent me next. He put me up at the York Hotel and I began a tour of the City, but mostly I kept my rig in sight at the Crossroads of the World, Times Square. Gotta clipping somewhere that tells about me driving my Moxiemobile there in the first Armistice Day Parade. Afterwards, I entertained hundreds of kids right there in the middle of the Square; showed them some tricks with my lariat; even lassoed some of those tads. It paid to play up to the youngsters; they sure could drink an amazing amount of Moxie. I guess the only people who weren't happy about me—except maybe the Coca Cola folks—were the street cleaners. If everyone drove the non-polluting kind of a horse I did, a lot of these 'white wings' would be put out of work.

"New York's Finest kept warning me to stay off Riverside Drive, inasmuch as no commercial vehicles were permitted on it. Well, as they say, I was full of Moxie and—since that Elks parade in Boston—my horse wasn't paying much attention to cops either, we simply decided to give those rich cats living in those fine mansions along the Drive something to look at beside the Hudson River. Lucky for me, we got away with it. Being any sort of a cowboy gets into the blood and stays there. Thirty years later, I checked into the York Hotel again, dressed western and wearing two guns on a good will tour to advertise the State of Arizona where I'd gone to live in 1938.

"I would've stayed in Gotham's bright lights longer, but Mr. Archer ordered me back to New England to cover county fairs and keep my horse as visible as possible. One day, while gallivanting around Cape Cod, I pulled into a fancy spread in Hyannisport. Some kids come out to see the horse and I gave them a ride on it. One of them I remember was named John Fitzgerald Kennedy.

"But beating the bushes in the boondocks wasn't the life to which I'd fast become accustomed. After Boston and New York, I'd begun to get bored. Still, I had my horse and the nights were

116

'Round the World Fliers.

California Frank's Rodeo.

Indian Princess and Friends.

At Braves Field in Boston.

118

nice. I stayed at the best hotels, parking my Essex alongside Rolls-Royce limousines and lots of those other fancy foreign motorcars. And there were scads of smiling senoritas. Some were school teachers; others were college girls; and I guess they thought I was somebody special—not just another plastic cowpoke like they have hanging around dude ranches these days.

"It didn't take a second invitation to get these lovelies out for a ride on my white charger. I mean I had to keep a sort of dance card in order to oblige them all. Yeah, I know what they say about a cowboy and his horse, but I don't think he was jealous. I guess he knew that it was really him and not me who was the big attraction. After all, when they took snapshots of us, he was the most important part of the picture.

"That big white bronco was lovely to look at up there on his sturdy Essex. He was really something to see if you didn't see him too suddenly—like the time when I was cruising alone through the White Mountains of New Hampshire one balmy moonlight night. Speeding over a hill, I met a car coming from the opposite direction. I don't know what the couple in it might have had on their minds but one thing was for sure, they didn't expect to see a tall white horse racing toward them like the wind. Whatever, the driver froze behind the wheel and that car kept coming right at me in the middle of the road.

"I whipped my steed to one side—way off the road, in fact—and ended up with the bumper of my rig wrapped around a tree. That couple who'd spooked my horse so bad didn't bother to stop—probably kept going even faster. I disentangled my guts from the pommel of the saddle; got the bumper straightened out the next day; and went on my way. You can be sure I didn't tell Mr. Archer about this near miss. He's heard enough about my escapades as it was.

"Frank Archer used to fire me every couple of weeks or so, then hire me back again. He wasn't much for nonsense though; had a reputation for being the first one in the office every day and the last one to leave; had a great sense of humor but could be hard as nails. Sometimes, when he'd start roaring around the office at me over something or other, everyone else would get scared, but I'd tell him off in a good-natured way and he'd laugh. I guess he knew I thought of him as a second dad. Still, I often wondered why he put up with me and gave me my head as often as he did.

"As I mentioned before, the general idea was for me and my

Moxiemobile to be seen around New England. My notions about being in the public eye didn't border on the spectacular, they jumped in with both feet. Risks were simply the frosting on the cake. Like the time I showed up at a fair in Maine. I don't remember if it was in Lewiston or Skowhegan. No matter, the folks who were there didn't forget me in a hurry; you can bet on that.

"What happened was I went up to the head of this fair and asked him how he'd like to have the fastest horse on earth perform for his patrons. 'Just how fast will this horse of yours go?' he asked. 'A mile a minute, easy,' I bragged. Well, I got him to look at my rig and he was sold. Moxie autos had done a mile a minute at county fairs a few years before, but horsemobiles were something else again, and this show promoter was no dummy. He was going to get a hair-raising exhibition mile at no expense to the fair. Just whose hair was going to get raised wasn't anticipated at the time.

"In those days race tracks were meant for horses only, not a horse on an automobile. They weren't banked for the sort of speed I could reach before going into a curve. Oh, I knew what I was doing. I'd been on such tracks with my horsemobile before. I'd come racing down the straightaways wide open; then I'd jam on the brakes and skid around the turns in a cloud of dust.

"So here we were at Skowhegan—or wherever. I sashayed my rig onto the oval, dismounted and bowed to the crowd; then I vaulted into the saddle and was off. The grandstand was loaded with people; hundreds more lined the rails around the track. Coming into the straightaway on the home stretch, I decided to give my audience an extra thrill this time. So I stood up on the saddle and put on my widest grin, one foot out behind me, one hand on the wheel and waving the other one at the spectators.

"The yokels in the grandstand got to their feet. The judge in the starter's box began waving a red flag frantically. Someone was clanging a bell. Everyone was pointing up at the sky. I had no idea why. I didn't worry about it either. I simply was aware that all this shouting was just for me; but I knew, too, that I had to get back into the saddle in order to make the turn after the finish line.

"I was dropping down onto my mount when something grazed the top of my head real hard. The folks standing up sank back into their seats with a groan that could be heard a mile. The judge fainted dead away. When I got back to the starter's box he was just coming to. 'Boy!' he exclaimed, 'I thought you hadn't seen it. You scared us half to death.' I was about to ask 'See what?' when

The Golden Chariot.

I looked up and saw the finish wire that had all but scalped me. That's when I felt like passing out myself. If that wire had caught me under the chin and taken my head off, the car would've kept going straight ahead and probably killed a lot of people.

"When Mr. Archer heard about the incident, he fired me immediately; but when the next day's papers came out with a big story about how his Moxie Boy gave those spectators the biggest thrill of the fair, the publicity Moxie got tickled him pink and he hired me back again. So I went on to more adventures for which I kept being fired and hired as usual.

"During June and July of 1930, I was driving a large, flatbed Moxie truck. I loved it. It was covered with gold leaf, had lights all around it, and I played tunes on a set of chimes hooked up to the horn button. In the back were a couple of big Moxie bottles. One was six feet tall and the other was eight feet. Inside these huge bottles, I carried advertising material and my luggage. I was driving through the Finger Lakes section of New York State when I was struck by another of my brilliant ideas. I wired Frances, a girl I had met on a date the year before in Buffalo. We were married in Montrose, Pennsylvania. The minister got a big kick out of it. He said we were the first couple who'd ever arrived in a golden chariot and he guessed there'd never be another.

"The last year I worked for Moxie was 1932, when again I had a horse. This one was made of aluminum and was mounted on a spiffy LaSalle chassis. I hear that it's still around and so am I!"

Mark Barker went on to become Moxo The Magician and once entertained 10,000 Navajo Indians who had never seen a white magician before. Moxo met many famous people, including that other magician, Blackstone; John Manville; Tom Mix; Harold Lloyd; and, of course, Senator Barry Goldwater. Ernie Pyle, in his book *Home Country* speaks highly of Moxo. "He was the damndest guy I ever ran on to."; wrote Ernie, "—he was like war music—infectious."

CHAPTER 9

Moxiemobiles
on Parade

Some folks think they remember seeing Moxie horsemobiles using Packard, Pierce-Arrow and Cadillac chassis. Although the three Cadillac-built LaSalles came close, only one car of this type (a super classic by today's standards) was used. It was a grand Silver Ghost Rolls-Royce. It is regrettable that this car did not survive. Given a few more years, this flagship of the Moxie Fleet might eventually have become enshrined in the Smithsonian Institution.

"I was the last private owner of the Rolls-Royce chassis on which a Moxie horse was mounted," says Frederick D. Roe of Holliston, Massachusetts. "It was complete except for the horse and the controls but at the time ('46) we had more Rolls-Royce cars and parts than we knew what to do with, so it finally went to a junkyard in Framingham (Massachusetts). I have a photo of it there."

In the background of this photograph is a shoe factory owned by R. H. Long, manufacturer of the Bay State automobile in the 1920s. The whereabouts of the horse from the chassis is a mystery, but it could be the one a New England collector obtained from a restaurant owner who may have used it for a display of some sort. This is a genuine, aluminum Moxie horse. It bears a patch where the steering column came down through its chest; and it can been seen that the lower parts of the legs were added.

"Back in the 1930s," wrote Robert Byrne of Brockton, Massachusetts, "I drove the Rolls-Royce, which was equipped with electric signs in bright colors and was always in demand for public appearances. We drivers were gaily attired as fox hunters and, in rainy weather, wore rubber capes for protection. Lollipops

Lady Moxiemobile drivers appeared only on signs.

Robert Byrne gassing up in Errol, New Hampshire, in the summer of 1935. This is a rare photograph showing the Rolls Royce Moxiemobile sporting white sidewall tires.

flavored with Moxie were handed out along the way for taste purposes. Moxie was considered an herb tonic in those days. That Rolls-Royce horse had frequent foul-ups. The fan belt was a segmented type and used to break. Replacement parts were hard to find.

"The restored horse looks nothing like the originals. They were pure white and had a smooth enamel surface. (The restored LaSalle's horse is a flocked buff.) To my knowledge, all the drivers were men. (Some of the Moxie advertising showed a woman in the saddle of the Rolls-Royce Moxiemobile.)

"Strangers were always stopping to take pictures of us on the horses. Others, mostly men, would holler 'Why don't you go out and get a job?' You mention that there are plans to sweeten the product. To sweeten Moxie would ruin it. I'm sure that Mr. Archer will turn over in his grave.

"I am enclosing an old newspaper clipping with a picture taken at the Boston *Post* Santa where free Moxie was always passed out to the workers. The Boston *Post* campaigned each year for money to help the poor and needy in the area. Clothes, toys and food were packed here by volunteers and distributed on Christmas Eve."

Anyone who heckled a Moxiemobile driver for not having a real job would probably have been hard-pressed if put in the saddle occupied by Nicholas "Bananas" Zaffiro. The Moxie Company didn't find Nick; he found it. One morning, in 1919, he happened to be at the corner of Haverhill and Beverly in Boston—where The Moxie Company was then located—and noticed a help-wanted sign. Sam Richards took Nick on temporarily as a machine operator.

But Nick stayed with The Moxie Company until 1951 when, according to Nick, they sold out to America Dry (Ginger Ale). "Would you believe," Nick went on to say, "there were guys working with me at the Moxie plant for all that time who never knew my real name? What happened was, I wasn't all that flush when I went to work for Moxie for that big fifteen bucks a week, so I did some moonlighting.

"One Saturday afternoon I was down at the market place with a pushcart selling fruit. Well, nobody ever told me there was anything funny about that but the word must've got out about it. Anyhow, when I showed up at my job with Moxie the next Monday morning, Arthur Penny—who was my foreman then—came by my machine and hollered 'Hey there, Joe Bananas!' So that's who I was from then on—except that sometimes they called me "Moxie Bananas.' "

For a few years, Nick didn't get to drive a Moxiemobile, but when he did it wasn't the joyride it might have seemed to some

MOXIE FOR POST SANTA WORKERS
Robert Byrne, the Moxieman, right, serving his product at the Boston Post workshop to one of Santa's volunteer workers. The beverage is donated free by the Moxie Company for the workers.

spectators. As if mastering the skill of handling such a vintage vehicle from high atop a horse wasn't enough, there were soul-trying hardships to endure such as coping with the wind, dust or rain, and the occasional unerring aim of some rotten kid with an even more rotten apple.

Nick Zaffiro's brief diary tells us something of the times in 1934. Gasoline was nineteen or twenty cents a gallon. He ate for an average of $3.00 a day and slept in hotels for $2.00 a night. These rates were somewhat less than what Charlie Hills paid back in the spring of 1899 when he was driving a Moxie Bottle Wagon. Surprising? Not to anyone who remembers The BIG Depression.

The restored LaSalle Moxiemobile at a Classic Car Club meet in North Easton, Massachusetts, in 1976. Robert Byrne (in the saddle) is discussing differences in driving mechanisms with Edwin C. White, president of the Simpson Spring Company of South Easton, a long-established distributor of Moxie.

It was a time when any sort of steady job was generally treated with considerable respect. Rather than go back to selling fruit again—such as apples on a street corner to folks who, out of genuine compassion, paid the outrageous price of five cents each for those excellent big apples—Nick hustled his 1929 LaSalle Moxiemobile from city to city with alacrity.

Leaving Boston on Monday, April 23rd, 1934, Nick showed off his mount, passed out advertising items and otherwise promoted Moxie in Springfield, Massachusetts; Waterbury and New Haven, Connecticut; New York City; Poughkeepsie, Milton, Kingston, Albany, Schenectady, Amsterdam, Utica, Syracuse and Binghamton, New York; Wilkes Barre, Williamsport, Hazelton and Allentown, Pennsylvania and arrived back in New York City

The Rolls-Royce Moxiemobile followed by two LaSalles. Drivers, from left to right: Mr. Leahy, Nicholas "Moxie Bananas" Zaffiro and Phil Segallo. The cowl sign on the Rolls-Royce had internal lighting. The large boulders in the background are some of the famous Roxbury Puddingstones.

Nick's kids, Diane and Tony, show off on Daddy's LaSalle Moxiemobile.

Nick Zaffiro poses as a Boston Gardens Moxie "butcher." Deep tray contained ice to keep bottles cool.

on May 19th.

On the road again, Nick visited twelve towns and cities in Pennsylvania, eight in Ohio, two in West Virginia; and took in Detroit, Michigan and Ft. Wayne, Indiana by June 25th. By the middle of July, he hit fourteen more places through West Virginia, Maryland, Pennsylvania, Connecticut, Massachusetts and Maine. From then until the middle of August—where Nick's diary for this trip ends—he made eighteen more stops.

All told, Nick traveled approximately 9000 miles and promoted Moxie along the open road, as well as in seventy-four towns and cities, in less than four months. Any present-day salesman—traveling in an air-conditioned sedan with an automatic transmission and cruise control—would be aghast at such an accomplishment. Why didn't Nick get a real job? Why not, indeed!

But Nick wasn't merely a Moxie Company employee, remember; he was an esteemed "associate." Today, he recalls his Moxie adventures with affectionate pride. "Every time we open a bottle of Moxie here in Revere, Massachusetts," says his daughter, Mrs. Diane Greene, "we have our expert taste-test it. To Dad, it's either 'perfect, good, fair, lousy' or, if it happens to remind him of the Moxie in 1919, 'a riot'!"

In 1978, the restored LaSalle Moxiemobile—perhaps the very one Nick used to drive—was in the annual Frontier Days Parade in Lisbon Falls, Maine. Over fifty entries were in this forty-five minute parade—not to mention all those contestants in the Miss Frontier Days Pageant with winners in four—count'em—four categories. Linda Barschdorf snapped a picture of Frank Anicetti, Jr. astride the Moxie horse. Frank, known in the area for Frank's Famous Frozen Fruited Flavors, makes Moxie ice cream; but then he also makes pumpkin and watermelon-flavored ice cream.

The Moxiemobile was exhibited at the celebrated Fryeburg (Maine) Fair, where it won a blue ribbon; and was also at the third annual Skowhegan (Maine) Log Day festival, which features such attractions as a Bean-Hole Dinner and a Spectacular Fireworks Show—as well as professional logging events. Log Days are observed to commemorate the last of the log drives down the Kennebec River, which were halted by legislative action.

The 1977 Memorial Day Parade in Laconia, New Hampshire, featured the Moxiemobile, which had previously been on display at Funspot in nearby Weirs Beach where thousands of visitors

Frank Anicetti (who signs his letters: A MOXIE DRINKER) in the saddle during the July, 1978, Frontier Days in Lisbon Falls, Maine.

"Look, Ma! No hands!" Bob LaBrie operates the Moxiemobile in a Fourth of July parade in Waterville, Maine. Bob is president of Eastern, Inc., the biggest Moxie bottler of them all. Besides being a big advertisement for Moxie, the "Horse" is somewhat of a hobby for Bob, his son, Paul, and Paul's brother-in-law, Jim Houghton, who has been the chief jockey.

On the Endicott Estate, East Dedham, Mass., summer of 1980.

stopped by for a good look and to exchange nostalgic stories with Bob LaBrie. Mr. LaBrie is president of Eastern, Inc. the world's largest bottler of Moxie formerly located in Lewiston, Maine, and is in charge of Moxiemobile appearances. Although Bob occasionally drives the horse, his son Paul's brother-in-law, Jim Houghton, is the chief jockey.

The Moxiemobile has also been in a Fourth of July parade in Waterville, Maine; at a Rotary Club auction in Damariscotta and Rotary Day in Brunswick, Maine. It is becoming an annual visitor at many of the above events and others; and has been requested for the Advertising and Sales Promotion Museum in conjunction with AD EXPO Week at the New York Coliseum.

Whether you're simply an antique-car buff, a Moxie Drinker, or both, the restored Moxiemobile is well worth going out of your way to see. For those of you who don't remember Moxie—but know what "moxie" means and may have been wondering how the word came about—we hope that this little book has been both enlightening and entertaining. As for you collectors of the odd and the interesting, you already know that the mere mention of Moxie can uncork memories in a way unmatched by any ordinary *memorabilia americana.*

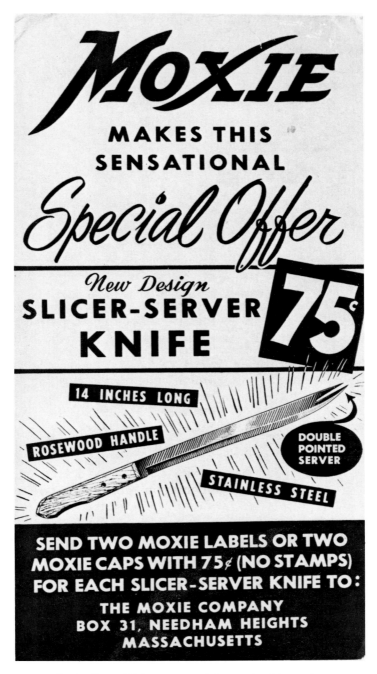

At Needham Heights, Moxie tried to cut it with premiums.

Epilogue

September 1981

Dear Reader:

An ancient philosophical poser goes something like this: If a tree falls in the forest, but nobody hears it, does it make a sound? A book is much the same. If one is written, but nobody reads it, well...? By reading THE MOXIE MYSTIQUE, you have become an important and ultimate part of the venture. Few books have been so exclusively by and for folks like yourself.

People have asked me why I wrote this book. A bewitching women in Salem, Massachusetts, was more to the point. She wanted to know whatever "possessed" me to do it. Actually, the idea had been haunting me for a long time. There was something mysterious about Moxie. The word "mystique" began to appear in dictionaries about the time I decided to delve into Moxie's past and find out just why the word "moxie" means what it does today.

Could childhood conditioning in Moxie country have influenced me? Maybe that pointing Moxie Man appeared from out of the past and made me do it. Whatever, the catalyst that initiated the whole intriguing investigation was my knowing Miles Harold Carpenter who had built a better Moxiemobile in 1917.

In the early 1960s, I wrote some articles about my friend, "Hal" Carpenter, which were published in *The Automobilist,* the house organ of an upstate New York antique car club. These pieces were eventually expanded to become OF HEART AND WHEELS, a book about the life of Mr. Carpenter, a fascinating man of many accomplishments, not the least of which were his many contributions to automobile design. Most of this autobiography first appeared serially throughout 1978 in *Antique Automobile.*

Alas! No horse molds in the basement.

One of the Myopia Club's colorful lables.

One of the chapters, "Horsing Around for Moxie," prompted Fred Roe of Holliston, Massachusetts, to write and tell me that he once owned the Rolls Royce Moxiemobile chassis. He had a file on Moxie and want to swop information. So Fred became one of the many Moxie buffs with whom I've had—and continue to have—an interesting variety of correspondence.

My first deliberate move to find out more about Moxie was to write to the Boston Chamber of Commerce, in 1962, to ask if they could put me in touch with someone who may have worked for The Moxie Company and might be willing to tell me something about it. To my surprise and delight, the folks in Boston informed me that The Moxie Company was still in business and gave me its Needham (Heights), Massachusetts, address—the Company long since having moved from Boston.

I wrote to The Moxie Company in Needham Heights and received a prompt and friendly reply from Orville Purdy, the general manager, who sent me two excellent old photographs of early Moxiemobiles, a couple of Moxie display cut-outs and a six-pack of Moxie. Mr. Purdy, in answer to my question about the Moxiemobiles, said that "With the exception of one LaSalle, all others have been discarded. The LaSalle is beyond use, but we are keeping it for sentimental reasons."

For the next few years, I busied myself writing stories for popular magazines while also working on OF HEART AND WHEELS. Toward the end of the 1960s I was on the road for a fiberglass products firm—which meant that I was away from home 'round the clock with no particular desire to sit down at a typewriter in some motel room after filling out endless reports of my long, long day's activities and planning for the morrow.

One evening, however, while studying a map of eastern Massachusetts, my eye was caught by some fine print that told me I should be passing through Needham the next day. Pass through it is something I did not do. I rushed into town and stopped at the first store that had a Moxie sign in the window. When I asked the way to the Moxie plant, I was told that the building was now occupied by a technical coatings firm.

"What happened to the LaSalle Moxiemobile?" I cried. "We don't know," I was told. "But the old aluminum horse molds are in the basement of the building. You could probably have them for the asking." I was too late. The Moxie Company had rescued them two weeks before I arrived.

Next, I was directed to the Myopia Club Bottling Company in nearby Islington. It was a very old plant. The machinery ran up hill and down, having adapted itself to the sagging floors. Nothing

Bottling plant is at the right.

Coming or going, you couldn't miss it.

seemed to be going on when I arrived, so I was able to have a friendly chat with the only person in the place at the time. He told me that he bottled Moxie for a local Moxie Drinkers club, but was willing to let me have a case of it. When I asked if he had any Moxie posters or other such items, he pulled a small crate from under a stairway and suggested that I open it. It looked as if it had come from King Tut's tomb.

Inside, neatly stacked between layers of yellowing wax paper, were some oval metal Moxie signs—the kind that are made to fasten to a wall and stick out so they can be read from either side. I was told that this crate of signs had been around the place since at least as far back as 1934. I left with three of these signs, several other Moxie advertising items, the case full of Moxie and an empty wooden case that was very old and too far gone to be sent out full of Moxie once more. My friend asked what I wanted that old box for. Wanted, indeed! I would have bought the whole plant if it had been for sale and I had had the price.

From the Myopia Club bottling plant, I was sent to other people in the vicinity who might be able to help me learn more about Moxie. After traipsing around Needham Heights, Islington and other little towns in the general environs of Boston, I completed my trip for the fiberglass people and came back home all steamed up about Moxie again.

I studied the pile of clippings, magazine articles and other things concerning Moxie that had been accumulating and wrote "Horsing Around for Moxie" which, as I mentioned earlier, was a chapter for OF HEART AND WHEELS. In 1969, I sent this to Frank Armstrong, who had taken Moxie to Atlanta, Georgia, the soft-drink capital of the world.

Mr. Armstrong kindly edited the chapter slightly to bring it up to date regarding the relocation of the company and added that they planned to restore the LaSalle Moxiemobile. I was pleased to learn that Mr. Armstrong was happy about what I was doing. So happy was he that he wrote me two letters on the same day giving me more news about Moxie and telling me how much he appreciated my "spreading the word."

Still, the idea of a Moxie book spinoff from OF HEART AND WHEELS hadn't surfaced sufficiently for me to get cracking on it. But the word was out that I was uncommonly interested in Moxie (some called it "freaked out") and more and more clippings about Moxie arrived, especially ones that showed how the popularity of the word "moxie" had carried over into the vocabularies of younger generations.

One of the items that was brought to my attention was an

article by Edna Hills Humphrey in the August, 1969, issue of *Yankee* magazine. It was titled "The Moxie Man" and related Mrs. Humphrey's father's adventures as a turn-of-the-century Moxie Bottle Wagon driver/salesman. So I wrote to *Yankee* after a few years and asked if they were ready for another article about Moxie. They replied that they were and, in June 1979, published "Moxie Memorabilia," in their popular "Antiques to look for" series.

At the time I queried *Yankee*, I also suggested Moxie articles to several other top magazines. As a result, many of them have already appeared and others are scheduled.

It was "Moxie Memorabilia," however, that brought the greatest reader response. (Mrs. Humphrey had told me to expect this.) Letters, phone calls, tape recordings, clippings and photographs came from folks as far away as California, Florida, Texas and Arizona. I had no idea there were so many people interested in Moxie. As letters flew back and forth and long distance phone calls were made—especially on weekends—we wrote the Moxie book, all my Moxie friends and I.

When our publisher gets the book in print, I'll put a case full of them in the back of my station wagon and take off to visit as many of my Moxie friends as possible. Recently, the Commonwealth of Virginia decided to make personalized automobile license plates available. Soon after this, I applied for a set to read M O X I E. Would you believe it? Somebody had beaten me to it. Too bad! But it does prove something. There sure are a lot of us around—and I hope you all are now more Moxie buffs than ever. If any of you would like to get in touch with me, I'll be delighted to hear from you. You can reach me by mail at 29 Franklin Road, Newport News, Va. 23601; or by phone 804-595-2043.

Cordially,

Frank N. Potter

Rare old Moxie bottle case with corners metal-bound rather than dovetailed.

Acknowledgments

The Moxie Company hadn't maintained any archives; and I wasn't able to find any one person who could give me even a rough idea of the whole Moxie story. For the past twenty years, however, a great many friendly people have furnished me with bits and pieces of the fascinating puzzle.

I simply can't remember all the folks I've met—and who've come to see me or written, phoned, dropped notes and things on my desk, and have helped me in other ways to learn more and more about Moxie.

I should have kept track of everyone but, in the beginning I really didn't know that I was going to write this book. So, if you were one of my helpers and your name doesn't appear below, drop me a line and I'll find a way to make it up to you. Be that as it may, I do remember most of you and I especially want to thank the following individuals and members of organizations for their generous assistance and friendly cooperation:

Mrs. Ivy W. Dodd and the *Courier-Gazette* in Rockland, Maine; and Mrs. Virginia S. McElwee (Granddaughter of Dr. Augustin Thompson, Moxie's founder) of Union, Maine, for much help regarding the early history of Moxie.

Miles Harold Carpenter of Wichita Falls, Texas, for telling me about his early experiences as a Moxie Drinker, and as a pioneer Moxiemobile builder.

Dallas Mundy of Williamsburg, Virginia, for his boyhood recollections of Moxie in the New England scene.

Mrs. Diane Greene of Revere, Massachusetts, and her father, Nicholas Zaffiro, for information about early Moxiemobile driving, a tape recording of a World War II phonograph record containing Moxie radio commercials, a film strip about Moxieland, much information about the Moxie Company from World War I to 1951 and a wealth of warm correspondence.

Frank A. Armstrong, President of the Moxie Company of Atlanta, Georgia, for his personal assistance and encouragement when I began writing about Moxie, and for the many illustrations he provided.

Carol Crouch, Secretary to Mr. Armstrong, for her continued cheerful help with details, and for supplying whatever items of interest she could find.

Philip Saltonstall Weld of Gloucester, Massachusetts, for his enthusiastic response with comments about Moxie and his OSTAR win with the trimaran "Moxie."

Jerry DeFuccio of New York City, for information about Moxie's appearance in *Mad* magazine.

Mrs. Edna Hills Humphrey of Mattapoisett, Massachusetts, for permission to quote extensively from her article "The Moxie Man" which appeared in *Yankee* magazine, and for putting me in touch with other Moxie friends.

Mr. and Mrs. James A. Todd of Silver Spring, Maryland, and Manchester, New Hampshire, for facts about their Moxie bottle house.

Mrs. Dorothy Robinson Wilson of Houston, Texas, for information about the early Moxie autos and the big Moxie bottle in the Pine Island Amusement Park in Manchester, New Hampshire, and for all her other many kindnesses.

Peter Harrigan, staff writer for the *New Hampshire Sunday News* in Manchester, New Hampshire, for information about, and photograph of, the Manchester Moxie bottle house.

Stanley K. Yost of Fort Myers, Florida, for information about, and picture of, the Haynes-Apperson horsemobile.

Loretta D. Balotte of Holden, Massachusetts, for letters about her uncle's harness shop horse and photographs of it.

Mark E. "MOXO" Barker of Mesa, Arizona, for the fantastic tale and photographs that became Chapter 8.

Frederick D. Roe of Holliston, Massachusetts, for considerable photographic assistance and for identifying several old Moxie vehicles—as well as providing illustrative material.

Robert V. Byrne of Brockton, Massachusetts, for correspondence concerning his days as a Moxiemobile driver and for several photographs.

George M. Blacker of Cheshire, Connecticut, for information about the "Moxie" phonograph record and for a photo of the label.

Merrill F. McLane of Bethesda, Maryland, for many Moxie clippings and for telling me about his Modox poster.

Doris L. Katz of Plymouth, Massachusetts, for asking me about her Moxie collectibles and telling me about her father, Frank Head, who was the Archer family's chauffeur.

Peter A. Trevera of Plantsville, Connecticut, for his comments about Moxie collectibles.

Pauline D. Higgins of Auburn, New Hampshire, for her efforts in finding information about Moxie for me.

George Comtois, Director of the Manchester Historical Association for finding a photograph of the Moxie bottle in Pine Island Park.

Iola Whitcomb of Rochester, New York, for the "Moxie" sheet music.

Orville S. Purdy of West Roxbury, Massachusetts, General Manager of the Moxie Company of Needham Heights, Massachusetts, for two wonderful photos of early Moxiemobiles, and for information about the Company.

Frank Anisetti and Linda Barschdorf of Lisbon Falls, Maine, for their enthusiastic interest in my Moxie writing, and for photographs of items in Frank's Moxiana collection.

Pete Herbert of Weirs Beach, New Hampshire, for telling me about the Moxiemobile's visit to FUNSPOT, and for the photo he kindly sent me.

Edwin C. White, President of the Simpson Spring Company in South Easton, Massachusetts, for putting me in touch with many former Moxiemobile drivers and for several useful photographs.

Bob and Paul LaBrie of Eastern, Inc. in Rochester, New Hampshire, for a great deal of help and information, many photographs and other illustrative material.

About the Author:

Since 1936, Frank N. Potter has been published, under several bylines, in a kaleidoscopic array of magazines and newspapers. Beyond becoming the country's leading Moxie expert (in 1979, the prestigious American Heritage Society expressed its appreciation to Mr. Potter for having brought the Moxie legend to its attention), he has achieved recognition as an automotive and aviation historian; and was awarded the M. J. Duryea Memorial Cup for his book, OF HEART AND WHEELS. His lively and authentic articles, as well as several chapters from his books, have appeared—and others are being scheduled for publication—in such magazines as: *Antique Automobile, Aviation Quarterly, Yankee* and *Modern Maturity.*